THE ABINGDON WORSHIP ANNUAL

2008

CONTEMPORARY & TRADITIONAL
RESOURCES FOR WORSHIP LEADERS

The

ABINGDON

WORSHIP

Annual

2008

EDITED BY MARY J. SCIFRES & B. J. BEU

Abingdon Press
Nashville

CONTENTS

Introduction ix

JANUARY

January 6, 2008 *Epiphany of the Lord* 1
January 13, 2008 *Baptism of the Lord* 6
January 20, 2008 *Second Sunday after the Epiphany* 10
January 27, 2008 *Third Sunday after the Epiphany* 15

FEBRUARY

February 3, 2008 *Transfiguration Sunday* 19
February 6, 2008 *Ash Wednesday* 25
February 10, 2008 *First Sunday in Lent* 30
February 17, 2008 *Second Sunday in Lent* 36
February 24, 2008 *Third Sunday in Lent* 41

MARCH

March 2, 2008 *Fourth Sunday in Lent/*
                 One Great Hour of Sharing 46
March 9, 2008 *Fifth Sunday in Lent* 50
March 16, 2008 *Palm/Passion Sunday* 55
March 20, 2008 *Holy Thursday* 60
March 21, 2008 *Good Friday/A Service of Tenebrae* 65
March 23, 2008 *Easter* 70
March 30, 2008 *Second Sunday of Easter* 74

APRIL

April 6, 2008 *Third Sunday of Easter* 78
April 13, 2008 *Fourth Sunday of Easter* 85
April 20, 2008 *Fifth Sunday of Easter* 89
April 27, 2008 *Sixth Sunday of Easter* 95

Contents

MAY

May 4, 2008 *Ascension Sunday/*
       Festival of the Christian Home 99
May 11, 2008 *Pentecost Sunday* 104
May 18, 2008 *Trinity Sunday* 110
May 25, 2008 *Second Sunday after Pentecost* 114

JUNE

June 1, 2008 *Third Sunday after Pentecost* 119
June 8, 2008 *Fourth Sunday after Pentecost* 124
June 15, 2008 *Fifth Sunday after Pentecost/*
      Father's Day 130
June 22, 2008 *Sixth Sunday after Pentecost* 135
June 29, 2008 *Seventh Sunday after Pentecost* 140

JULY

July 6, 2008 *Eighth Sunday after Pentecost* 144
July 13, 2008 *Ninth Sunday after Pentecost* 148
July 20, 2008 *Tenth Sunday after Pentecost* 152
July 27, 2008 *Eleventh Sunday after Pentecost* 156

AUGUST

August 3, 2008 *Twelfth Sunday after Pentecost* 161
August 10, 2008 *Thirteenth Sunday after Pentecost* 165
August 17, 2008 *Fourteenth Sunday after Pentecost* 169
August 24, 2008 *Fifteenth Sunday after Pentecost* 174
August 31, 2008 *Sixteenth Sunday after Pentecost* 178

SEPTEMBER

September 7, 2008 *Seventeenth Sunday after Pentecost* ... 183
September 14, 2008 *Eighteenth Sunday after Pentecost* ... 187
September 21, 2008 *Nineteenth Sunday after Pentecost* ... 191
September 28, 2008 *Twentieth Sunday after Pentecost* 195

OCTOBER

October 5, 2008 *Twenty-first Sunday after Pentecost/World*
      Communion Sunday 199
October 12, 2008 *Twenty-second Sunday after Pentecost* ... 204

Contents

October 19, 2008 *Twenty-third Sunday after Pentecost* 208
October 26, 2008 *Twenty-fourth Sunday after Pentecost/*
                    Reformation Sunday 213

NOVEMBER

November 2, 2008 *Twenty-fifth Sunday after Pentecost* 218
November 9, 2008 *Twenty-sixth Sunday after Pentecost* . . . 221
November 16, 2008 *Twenty-seventh Sunday after Pentecost* . . . 226
November 23, 2008 *Reign of Christ/Christ the King* 231
November 27, 2008 *Thanksgiving Day* 236
November 30, 2008 *First Sunday of Advent* 241

DECEMBER

December 7, 2008 *Second Sunday of Advent* 246
December 14, 2008 *Third Sunday of Advent* 253
December 21, 2008 *Fourth Sunday of Advent* 257
December 24, 2008 *Christmas Eve* 262
December 28, 2008 *First Sunday after Christmas* 266

Contributors 271
Scripture Index 275
Communion Liturgy Index 278

INTRODUCTION

To worship God is an awesome experience. To lead others in the worship of God is a humbling opportunity to facilitate this experience. To help pastors and worship leaders accomplish this daunting task, we offer *The Abingdon Worship Annual 2008* as a resource and partner in your planning process. The task of planning worship can be filled with joy and excitement; it can also be plagued with the worries of deadlines and multiple responsibilities. In order to ease some of those worries, this resource offers worship words for each Sunday of the lectionary year, along with suggestions for many of the "high" holy days. Each entry provides suggestions that follow an order of service that may be adapted to address your specific worship practice and format. Feel free to reorder or pick and choose the various resources to fit the needs of your worship services and congregations.

The Abingdon Worship Annual 2008 moves in a new direction from previous volumes. Each week's entry provides a specific thematic focus arising from one or more of the week's scriptures. That theme, along with corresponding scripture imagery, is then carried out through each of the suggested prayers and litanies. For those who are working with contemporary worship services, alternative ideas for those settings are offered for each service as well. Each entry includes a Call to Worship, Opening Prayer, Prayers of Confession or Unison Prayers, Responses to the Word, Offertory or Communion Resources, and Benedictions. Additional ideas are also provided throughout this resource. We have ordered each day's suggestions to fit the basic pattern of Christian worship, reflecting a flow that leads from a time of gathering and praise, into a time of receiving and responding to the word, and ending with a time of sending forth. The Praise Sentences and Contemporary Gathering Words fit the spontaneous and informal nature of many nontraditional worship styles and easily fit into the time for gathering and praise.

In response to requests from many of our readers, we have provided a number of communion liturgies as well. Most follow the pattern of the Great Thanksgiving; others are Prayers of Preparation and Consecration for the celebration of the Eucharist. Consult the index for a listing of these many communion resources, and feel free to use them interchangeably throughout the corresponding seasons. For instance, the communion service for Transfiguration Sunday could be used at any time during the season of Epiphany.

The Abingdon Worship Annual complements several other resources from Abingdon Press. As you plan lectionary-based worship, you will find *The Abingdon Preaching Annual* an invaluable help. Worship planners and preachers can also rely upon *Prepare! A Weekly Worship Planbook for Pastors and Musicians* or *The United Methodist Music and Worship Planner,* all published by Abingdon Press, for excellent music suggestions of hymns, praise songs, vocal solos, and choral anthems. Together, these three resources provide the words, the music, and the preaching guidance to plan integrated and coordinated worship services.

All contributions in *The Abingdon Worship Annual* are based upon readings from *The Revised Common Lectionary.* As you begin your worship planning, we encourage you to spend time with the scriptures for the day, reflecting upon them thoughtfully and prayerfully. Review the thematic ideas suggested in this resource and then read through the many words for worship that speak to the theme in reflection of scripture. Listen for the words that speak to you. Let this resource be the starting point for your worship planning, letting the Spirit guide you and allowing God's word to flow through you. Worship that arises from careful and caring planning honors the God who gave such careful planning to our creation and gives such caring attention to our world and our needs.

Many litanies, prayer, and calls to worship in *The Abingdon Worship Annual 2008* intersperse direct quotations from scripture with lines of text from other sources. In order to focus on the poetic nature of worship words, and to facilitate the ease of use with this resource, we do not indicate these direct quotations with quotation marks.

Since the contributing authors represent a wide variety of denominational and theological backgrounds, the words before you will vary in style and content. Feel free to combine or adjust the words within these pages to fit the needs of your congregation and the style of your worship services. (Notice the reprint permission for worship given on the copyright page of this book.) Trust God's guidance, and enjoy a wonderful year of worship and praise with your congregations! We wish you God's blessings as you seek to share Christ's word and offer experiences of the Holy Spirit in your work and worship!

Mary J. Scifres and B. J. Beu, Editors

JANUARY 6, 2008

Epiphany of the Lord
Joanne Carlson Brown

COLOR
White

SCRIPTURE READINGS
Isaiah 60:1-6; Psalm 72:1-7; Ephesians 3:1-12; Matthew 2:1-12

THEME IDEAS
In the Northern Hemisphere, we are experiencing the darkness of midwinter. Days are short and nights long. But there are other forms of darkness—poverty, war, injustice, oppression, hatred, prejudice, fear—forms that also affect us just as they did the people of biblical times. In these passages, light breaks through the darkness: a prophet calls us to arise and see the light of liberation and peace, reconciliation and joy; the psalmist prays for a ruler who will light the way of his people with righteousness, prosperity, and an end to oppression and injustice. The writer of Ephesians lights the way through mystery, with a message of the good news of Christ Jesus; and the Magi follow the light of a star, finding more than they were looking for, to return home transformed.

INVITATION AND GATHERING

Call to Worship

Arise; shine, for your light has come!
We are called out of our darkness into light.
Lift up your eyes and look around.
We rejoice in the gift of light.
Come let us worship the God of light and joy and peace.
We come to kneel at the cradle of the babe,
the light incarnate.

Opening Prayer

God of promise and light,
open our eyes this morning,
that we may see your light in the darkness.
Open our hearts,
that we may perceive your promises
of justice and righteousness
fulfilled in the babe of Bethlehem.
May we, like the Magi,
have a star to guide us
on our journey quest
to find the one who will truly set us free.
May this time of worship
bring us closer to you,
that the good news
of the birth of light and love
will transform our lives. Amen.

PROCLAMATION AND RESPONSE

Prayer of Confession

Ever-patient God,
we are a people who live in thick darkness.
We stumble around
bombarded by news of war and poverty,
famine and genocide,
injustice and oppression.

The maelstrom of things and issues
   and people of the dark,
      can overwhelm and paralyze us.
Help us be people of the light,
   shining your light of righteousness, peace, and joy
      into all the dark places of our lives and world.
Unlock the mystery and glory
   of the babe born in Bethlehem.
Turn our aimless wanderings
   into a journey of purpose
      guided by your star.
Let the light break into our lives and our world,
   and transform us into people of the light.

Words of Assurance

As certain as the dawn follows the night,
   so is the promise of God's forgiveness
      and love for us all.
Arise and Shine.
Follow the star.
Find the light of the world born in Bethlehem ...
   and be transformed from darkness into light.

Passing the Peace of Christ

Lift your eyes and look around.
The light of the babe of Bethlehem
   shines from the face of each one here.
Let us now greet that light,
   rejoice that we are here together,
   and pass the peace of Christ,
   our joy and our hope.

Invitation to the Word/Sermon

Open our hearts and minds to the light of your word
   read and preached.

Response to the Word/Sermon

We rejoice in the mystery
   made plain through the good news

of the babe of Bethlehem.
May this good news transform us and guide us
as we seek to follow the star of love and light.

THANKSGIVING AND COMMUNION

Invitation to the Offering

We have seen the light of the world.
We have been called to follow the star of promise.
Like the Magi,
let us bring our gifts to honor the babe of Bethlehem
and bring the light to all the dark places
in our community and our world.

Offering Prayer

God of light and promise,
we bring our gifts
to further your work in a dark world.
May they bring your light
to those overwhelmed
by darkness, pain, and loneliness.
Accept these gifts of money and time,
indeed, the gift of our very selves.
Let them shine for all to see,
and be brought into the sphere of your love
and righteousness.

SENDING FORTH

Benediction

Arise, and go forth to shine for all the world to see.
**We go to spread the good news of light and love,
righteousness and justice.**
Go now and follow the star
that will guide you on your journey
this week, this year, and forever.
As the Magi of old,

**we go forth in trust and excitement,
transformed in the presence
of the child of light.**
May the blessing of the God of light
rest upon you and fill you with light.
Amen.

CONTEMPORARY OPTIONS

Contemporary Gathering Words

Light has broken in on the darkness of the world!
Can you see it? Can you feel it?
Open the eyes of your heart and light the light within.
There is a star beckoning us to follow.
Let's go and see where it leads us today in worship.
Let's see where it leads us tomorrow
    as we go about our day, our week,
        and the rest of our lives.

Praise Sentences

Arise and shine, for your light has come.
Lift up your eyes and look around.
Praise the God of promise and light and love.
Praise the God of the guiding star.

JANUARY 13, 2008

Baptism of the Lord
Robert Blezard

COLOR
White

SCRIPTURE READINGS
Isaiah 42:1-9; Psalm 29; Acts 10:34-43; Matthew 3:13-17

THEME IDEAS
Jesus' baptism in the Jordan, at the hands of John the Baptizer, publicly identifies Jesus as the Christ—the Messiah, the Anointed, the Chosen One of God. This baptism also marks the beginning of the ministry for the long-awaited Messiah, whose coming is foretold in the Isaiah reading. As Peter explains the Acts passage, we can trust in the saving work of Jesus the Christ.

INVITATION AND GATHERING

Call to Worship (Acts 10)
Incline your ear! Hear the good news!
  God's Messiah is Jesus of Nazareth.
God has chosen us as witnesses.
  God's Anointed is Jesus of Nazareth.

Open your hearts to receive his word.
God's Ordained is Jesus of Nazareth.
He is preached and glorified in prayer and song.
God's Chosen One is Jesus of Nazareth.
Jesus of Nazareth is the Christ!
Jesus the Christ is Lord of all.

Opening Prayer (Isaiah 42)
Holy, merciful, loving God,
    we, your children,
        long for your presence.
We, who sit in darkness,
    have hope in you.
By the light of your Christ,
    the presence of your Anointed One,
        illuminate our lives.
Let your Chosen One, our Savior,
    dispel our blindness,
    open our eyes,
    free us from the dungeons of despair,
    and open every prison of oppression.

PROCLAMATION AND RESPONSE

Prayer of Confession (Isaiah 42)
O God of light, God of glory,
    you gave us the breath of life,
    you gave us your Spirit,
    and then you called us to be your people.
By baptism you adopted us as your children,
    to be a light to the nations,
    to be salt of the earth.
We have failed to live as we should,
    putting our earthly desires and selfish wants
        ahead of your command to love and to serve.
For all the sin that permeates our lives,
    we beg your mercy and pray your pardon.

Words of Assurance (Acts 10)

Hear the words that soothe the troubled soul.
In mercy, God has given us his Son Jesus Christ,
that all who believe in him receive forgiveness of sin
through his name.

Response to the Word/Sermon (Isaiah 42)

You have taken us by the hand, O God,
and kept us for your own.
You know us better than we know ourselves.
Our doubts, our fears, our weaknesses
are not hidden from your sight,
nor our strengths, our potentials, our joys.
May your Spirit work within us
to spark and kindle our faith,
to give us courage and vanquish our fear,
that we may arise as your people,
as your hands and your eyes in the world.
Amen.

THANKSGIVING AND COMMUNION

Call to Prayer (Acts 10)

As a father inclines to the words of his daughter,
our God listens to the deepest prayers of our hearts.
As a mother responds to her son's cries of pain,
our God hears the distress of our souls.
Let us bring our cares and joys before our loving God,
whose patience is broad and whose mercy is deep.

Offering Prayer (Psalm 29, Acts 10)

Majestic God, creative God,
we stand in awe of your strength,
your voice resounding on earth,
calling your creatures to obedience
and shaping them by your command.
May your word challenge us to arise,
to witness to your strength and love,

to preach the gospel of Jesus the Christ,
    that Christ is Lord of all,
the only name under heaven that saves.

SENDING FORTH

Benediction (Psalm 29)
    The Lord gives strength to the people of God!
    The Lord blesses them with holy peace!
    Depart with joy and courage.
    Depart with confidence and peace.
    Amen.

CONTEMPORARY OPTIONS

Contemporary Gathering Words (Acts 10, Matthew 3)
    God's Spirit is among us,
        calling us to faith,
        challenging us to arise,
        emboldening us to serve.
    God's Spirit has descended upon us like a dove,
        marking us as God's own,
        to be light and salt.

Praise Sentences (Psalm 29)
    What can compare to the strength of our God?
    God's power to create beats our power to destroy.
    God's power to forgive beats our power to condemn.
    God's power to love beats our power to hate.
    God's power to invite beats our power to exclude.
    God's power to heal beats our power to hurt.
    God's power to transform beats our power to stagnate.
    What can compare to the strength of our God?

JANUARY 20, 2008

Second Sunday after the Epiphany

Mary J. Scifres

COLOR

Green

SCRIPTURE READINGS

Isaiah 49:1-7; Psalm 40:1-11; 1 Corinthians 1:1-9; John 1:29-42

THEME IDEAS

God's call emerges as a dominant theme in today's readings. Isaiah proclaims that God's call came even before he was born (Isaiah 49:1b). John clarifies his prophetic calling to proclaim the coming of Christ (John 1:31b). Jesus invites John and others to "Come and see" (John 1:39). Andrew calls to his brother Simon, "We have found the Messiah" (John 1:41b), and brings Simon to Jesus. Jesus calls Simon to discipleship and renames him Cephas (Peter). As God has called disciples since the beginning of time, so Christ calls us through these many scriptures.

INVITATION AND GATHERING

Call to Worship (Psalm 40, John 1)
Come and see, for Christ is here.
Come and see the glories of God.
Come and hear, for Christ is calling.
Come and hear the word of the Lord.
Come and know the love of God.
Come and know the mercy of Christ.
Come and worship the Giver of Life!

Opening Prayer (1 Corinthians 1)
Faithful, loving God,
strengthen us in this hour.
Nurture our lives,
and bless us, we pray.
You have given us all that we need
to be your church.
Help us trust that your grace is sufficient.
As we worship,
let your Spirit move through us,
and open our hearts and minds
to hear your call.
With gratitude and trust, we pray. Amen.

PROCLAMATION AND RESPONSE

Prayer of Confession (Psalm 40, 1 Corinthians 1)
Merciful God,
you know our strengths
and our weaknesses.
You know where we most need to listen,
and where we most need to act.
Forgive us for speaking
when you need us to be silent.
Forgive us for sitting still
when you need us to move forward.

Wash over us with your mercy and grace,
    that we may find strength,
        even in our weakness.
Call to us with persistence and trust,
    that we may answer your call
        and live as your disciples. Amen.

Words of Assurance (Psalm 40, 1 Corinthians 1)

Know, my friends, that God has drawn us out
    of the sins of our lives,
and has strengthened us
    with Christ's steadfast love.
We proclaim God's faithfulness in this assurance:
    in the name of Jesus Christ,
        we are forgiven!

Response to the Word/Sermon (1 Corinthians 1, Psalm 40)

Strengthen us, O God,
    to heed the calling
        you have placed in our lives.
Encourage us to trust the voices and instructions
    that make us who we are
        as disciples of your Son.
Let your unending love,
    and constant faithfulness,
        shine through us,
        that we may truly be your people
           on this earth.

Call to Prayer (Psalm 40)

Wait patiently for God, who hears our cries.
Trust in the One who calls us each by name.
Let us listen and wait in our time of prayer.
(A time for silent prayer may follow.)

THANKSGIVING AND COMMUNION

Offering Prayer (Psalm 40, Isaiah 49)
Wondrous God,
    we delight in your abundant gifts
      and receive your bounty with thanks.
As we share a portion of your abundance,
    transform our offerings,
      that they may be your promise of hope
      to a world in need.
Transform our lives,
    that we may walk in your ways
      and be a light to all the world. Amen.

SENDING FORTH

Benediction (1 Corinthians 1)
We have been strengthened by Christ and blessed by God.
**Every gift, every talent, everything that we need
is here in the body of Christ.**
God has called; we have listened.
We go forth in response to God's call!

CONTEMPORARY OPTIONS

Contemporary Gathering Words (Isaiah 49)
Listen from far and near.
Listen with the earth and the sea.
Listen, for God is speaking—
    speaking of light and life.
Listen, for Christ is calling—
    calling to one and all.
Listen for the voice of the Spirit—
    the Spirit that gathers us here.
Listen, listen, listen.
We are the ones called to bring light
    to the nations on earth.

Praise Sentences (1 Corinthians 1, John 1)

Give thanks to our God, who is loving and just!
Blessed be the lamb of God!
Come and see: Christ is here!

JANUARY 27, 2008

Third Sunday after the Epiphany

B. J. Beu

COLOR
Green

SCRIPTURE READINGS
Isaiah 9:1-4; Psalm 27:1, 4-9; 1 Corinthians 1:10-18; Matthew 4:12-23

THEME IDEAS
Themes of light and darkness focus the readings from Isaiah, Psalm 27, and Matthew's Gospel. In the midst of loss (destruction of one's homeland, the death of John the Baptist), hope is not lost. God's light shines in the darkness: "The people who walked in darkness have seen a great light; those who lived in a land of deep darkness— on them light has shined" (Isaiah 9:2).

INVITATION AND GATHERING

Call to Worship (Isaiah 9, Psalm 27, Matthew 4)
The Lord is our light and our salvation.
   Whom shall we fear?
The Lord sets us high on a rock, above our enemies.

The Lord shelters us in our day of trouble.
We, who have walked in darkness, have seen a great light.
**We, who have dwelled in a land of deep darkness,
on us, light has shined.**
The Lord is our light and our salvation.
Whom shall we fear?

Opening Prayer (Isaiah 9, Psalm 27)
God of radiant light,
shine into our lives,
and disperse the darkness
that dims our vision;
shine into our world,
and cast out the fears
that long have chained us;
shine into our worship,
that we may be a people
of your hope and promise.
Amen.

PROCLAMATION AND RESPONSE

Prayer of Confession (Psalm 27, Matthew 4)
Glorious God, our light, and our salvation,
too often we have been afraid.
We behold the beauty of your dwelling place,
and feel unworthy to meet you there.
We view the cleft in the rock,
where you would hide us from our enemies,
and we shrink from its dizzying height.
When your prophets are arrested and put to death,
we hide in the darkness,
rather than proclaim the dawning
of your great light.
Forgive our foolishness.
Guide our timid feet,
And do not forsake us,
O God of our salvation! Amen.

Words of Assurance (Isaiah 9)

The gloom and grief of the former times
  have passed away.
The hope and glory of the latter times
  have washed over us like the tide of the sea.
We, who once sat in darkness,
  and who now behold the glory of God's holy light,
  find forgiveness in God's promises,
    and find joy in God's redeeming love.

Response to the Word/Sermon (Isaiah 9, Matthew 4)

Radiant Light,
  shine into our hearts,
    that we might dwell in darkness no longer;
  illumine your words,
    that our lives might reflect your Word made flesh;
  draw us from the shadow of death
    into the dawning of your light and life,
      through Jesus Christ, our eternal Light. Amen.

Call to Prayer (Psalm 27)

Seek the One who shines light into our darkness.
Trust the One who is the stronghold of our lives.
Call on the One who breaks the rod of the oppressor
  and who brings warmth and light in the midst
    of winter.
(A time for silent prayer or Prayer of the People may follow.)

THANKSGIVING AND COMMUNION

Offering Prayer (Isaiah 9, Matthew 4)

Gracious God,
  we thank you for this day—
    a day blessed with light and joy,
    a day blessed with hope and abundance.
May these offerings
  bring light to those who dwell still in darkness,
    or who cower in the shadow of death.

Bless our lives to your service,
in the name of your Son,
who calls us to follow him
and share your light with others. Amen.

SENDING FORTH

Benediction (1 Corinthians 1)

Be a people of the light.
Christ's light shines upon us.
Be a people of the light.
Christ's light dispels our fear!
Be a people of the light.
Christ's light blesses us with joy!
Go; be a people of the light.

CONTEMPORARY OPTIONS

Contemporary Gathering Words (Isaiah 9, Matthew 4)

When will the night be over?
God's light is shining.
When will the darkness end?
God's light is shining.
When will the path to Christ be clear?
God's light is shining.
God's light is shining.
God's light is shining, indeed!

Praise Sentences (1 Corinthians 1, John 1)

The Lord is my light and my salvation!
Christ is my light and my salvation!
Praise the light!
Praise the light!
Praise the light!

FEBRUARY 3, 2008

Transfiguration Sunday
Mary J. Scifres

COLOR
White

SCRIPTURE READINGS
Exodus 24:12-18; Psalm 99; 2 Peter 1:16-21; Matthew 17:1-9

THEME IDEAS
The dazzling brightness of God shines through our scriptures today. The light of Christ that shone in the darkness the promised prophetic Advent now shines from on high. The morning star has arisen and God's promises find fulfillment in Jesus, the Light of the World.

INVITATION AND GATHERING

Call to Worship (2 Peter 1, Matthew 17)
The light of the Lord is shining with love.
Rise in our hearts, Bright Morning Star.
God calls to us now, saying, "Be not afraid."
Give peace in our lives, O Promised One.
Come to the mountain and gaze at the glory.
Shine in our lives, Light of the World!

Opening Prayer (Psalm 99)
> Majestic God,
> > shine upon us
> > > with your glorious love;
> > shine through us
> > > with your brilliant grace.
> As we worship together,
> > reveal your truth to us,
> > that we might see and live
> > > the paths of discipleship
> > > you set before us.

PROCLAMATION AND RESPONSE

Prayer of Confession (Psalm 99)
> Forgive us, O God,
> > when we stumble in the darkness
> > and turn away from your face.
> Strengthen us to walk in your brightness
> > and live in your ways.
> Enlighten the shadows
> > that keep us from growing
> > in your love and light.
> Shower us with your grace,
> > that we might shine as your people
> > upon this earth.

Words of Assurance (2 Peter 1)
> We are all God's beloved children.
> Through the grace of Christ, we are forgiven!

Response to the Word/Sermon (Matthew 17)
> God of the Ages,
> > lift us up
> > > to face your brilliance
> > > and your truth.
> Give us the courage and hope
> > to live as your people—
> > > a people of light and love.

THANKSGIVING AND COMMUNION

The Great Thanksgiving (An Act of Preparation for Holy Communion)

    The Lord be with you.
    And also with you.
    Come to the mountain of the Lord.
    We come to see God's glory.
    Lift up your hearts.
    We lift them up to the Lord.
    Let us give thanks to the Lord our God.
    It is right to give our thanks and praise.

    It is right, and a good and joyful thing,
        always and everywhere, to give thanks to you,
        Almighty God, creator of heaven and earth.
    Out of nothing, you created all that is,
        mighty mountains and quiet lakes.
    Out of dust, you formed us in your image,
        and breathed into us the breath of life.
    You called us again and again to your holy mountain,
        to worship and praise your holy name.
    You led your people to Mount Sinai,
        giving your commandments,
        and creating a covenant people.
    When we strayed and lost our way
        in the wilderness of life,
        you led us like a pillar of light.
    You fed us with the bread of life,
        and nourished us with the law and the prophets.
    In the fullness of time, you sent your Son, Jesus Christ,
        to be the light that guides us
        at all times and in all places.
    From mighty mountains, he shone with your glory.
    From quiet lakesides, he preached your word
        and taught us your ways.
    With gentle hands of healing and harsh words of justice,

Jesus invited all people to live in your love
and to walk in your light.
Into this covenant community, we have come
to be your people and to praise your name.
And so, with your people on earth,
and all the company of heaven,
we praise your name and join their unending hymn.
> **Holy, holy, holy Lord, God of power and might,**
> **heaven and earth are full of your glory.**
> **Hosanna in the highest.**
> **Blessed is the one who comes**
> **in the name of the Lord.**
> **Hosanna in the highest.**

Holy are you, and blessed is the Light of the World,
Christ Jesus.
When you sent Christ to this earth,
he walked dusty roads and climbed high mountains,
showing us your presence in a myriad of ways.
By Christ's grace and glory,
we are invited into your presence,
rescued from our sins,
and led into the light of your glory.
With Christ's call in our lives,
we are invited into your covenant community,
to live as a light to the nations.
With joy and gratitude, we remember that night
in which Jesus took the bread, broke it,
gave it to the disciples and said:
"Take, eat, this is the bread of life, given for you.
Do this in remembrance of me."
After supper, Jesus took the cup, blessed it
and gave it to the disciples and said,
"Drink from this, all of you.
This is my life for the new covenant,
poured out for you and for many
for the forgiveness of sins.

Do this, as often as you drink it,
    in remembrance of me."
And so, in remembrance of these,
    your mighty acts of love and grace,
    we offer ourselves in praise and thanksgiving.
As your covenant people and as reflections of your glory,
    in union with Christ's love for us,
    we proclaim the mystery of faith.
    Christ has died.
    Christ is risen.
    Christ will come again.

Communion Prayer (Epiphany, Transfiguration)

Pour out your Holy Spirit
    on all gathered here,
    that we might be your light in the world.
Pour out your Holy Spirit
    on these gifts of bread and wine,
    that we might be infused with the gift
    of your nourishing guidance.
Transform us with your nourishing grace,
    even as we eat of this bread
    and drink of this wine.
Transfigure us to be your presence in the world,
    even as we are redeemed and reclaimed
    by your great love.
By your Spirit, make us one with Christ,
    one with each other,
    and one in ministry to the world,
    until Christ comes in final victory,
    and we feast at the heavenly banquet.
Through Jesus Christ,
    with the Holy Spirit in your holy Church,
    all honor and glory is yours, almighty God,
    now and forever more.
    Amen.

Giving the Bread and Cup

(The bread and wine are given to the people, with these or other words of blessing.)
The life of Christ, living in you.
The light of Christ, shining through you.

SENDING FORTH

Benediction (Matthew 17)

Come down from the mountain with mountainlike faith.
Walk on God's paths as bright, shining lights.
Live in God's ways with faith, hope, and love.
Go into the world transformed and renewed!

CONTEMPORARY OPTIONS

Contemporary Gathering Words (Matthew 17)

Come up to the mountain of God.
Look upon the brightness of Christ.
Breathe in the hope of salvation.
Rejoice! The Spirit is here!

Praise Sentences (Psalm 99, 2 Peter 1)

Worship the Lord, the Light of the World!
Praise to Christ, the Star of our lives!
Worship the Lord, the Light of the World!

FEBRUARY 6, 2008

Ash Wednesday
Mary J. Scifres

COLOR
Purple or Gray

SCRIPTURE READINGS
Joel 2:1-2, 12-17; Psalm 51:1-17; 2 Corinthians 5:20b–6:10;
Matthew 6:1-6, 16-21

THEME IDEAS
Today's scriptures point to joy! Read carefully and you
will see a call to repent and to return to God. God, in
turn, promises to restore to us the joy of our salvation
(Psalm 51:12a). For some reason, Ash Wednesday traditions tend to ignore the promise of joy in this day's scriptures. The end of the Lenten journey is not death, but
rather resurrection. With resurrection hope, these readings remind us of a love that reconciles us inseparably
with God. Ash Wednesday and Lent call us to turn back
to the One who offers us all the treasure we will
ever need.

INVITATION AND GATHERING

Call to Worship (Joel 2, 2 Corinthians 5)
"Return to me!"
    Christ calls and we listen.

"Return to me!"
Christ calls, and we hear.
"Return to me!"
Christ calls, and we respond.
"Return to me!"
Christ calls, and we turn ...
toward love, toward joy, toward God.

Opening Prayer (Joel 2, Psalm 51)
O Promised One,
  speak to our hearts.
Call us forth into hope and joy.
Call us into the repentance
  that turns our hearts and our love toward you
    and toward your world.
Call to us,
  and we will listen.
Call to us,
  and we will hear.
Call to us,
  and we will respond.
Call to us,
  and we will return to love,
  to joy, to you. Amen.

PROCLAMATION AND RESPONSE

Call to Confession (Joel 2)
Come to God with open hearts and honest words.
Fear no punishment here,
  for our God relents from punishment.
Speak truth in your heart,
  for our God is full of grace and mercy,
    slow to anger, and eager to love.

Prayer of Confession (Joel 2, Psalm 51, 2 Corinthians 5)
Gracious God,
  we have not always trusted in your grace.

In times of sin and doubt,
  some of us fear your judgment.
In times of confusion and chaos,
  some of us expect your dictatorlike guidance.
In times of anger and disappointment,
  some of us offer only division and hatred.
Forgive us when we are not people of your grace.
Restore us to the joy of our salvation,
  that we may rejoice in your love
    and remember your grace.
Reconcile us with your mercy and love,
  that we might truly be your righteousness in the world.
Teach us your wisdom,
  that we might reflect your abundant love
    and gracious mercy.
In Christ's name, we pray. Amen.

Words of Assurance (2 Corinthians 5–6)

Rejoice, my friends!
For now is the day of salvation!
In Christ Jesus, we are reconciled to God.
Amen and amen.

Invitation to the Word

Listen, as Christ calls to us.
  O God, let us hear joy and gladness!
Hear, as Christ calls to us.
  O God, teach us the wisdom of grace!
Respond, as Christ calls to us.
  O God, restore to us the joy of our salvation!

THANKSGIVING AND COMMUNION

Invitation to Distribution of Ashes

Hear, O people of God,
  Christ calls to us with mercy and grace.
Let us respond with hope and joy.
Let us listen for the true wisdom God offers.

Let us return to God,
　　for in Christ we are reconciled
　　　　and made one with our Maker.
Hear, O people of God,
　　Christ calls to us with mercy and grace.

Response to Word/Sermon
　　Merciful God,
　　　　with open hearts,
　　　　　　we desire to live in your grace.
　　Speak to us with wisdom and mercy.
　　Call to us with patience and perseverance.
　　As you speak, and as you call,
　　　　we will respond.
　　As we offer ourselves to you,
　　　　transform us
　　　　　　that we may be your righteousness.
　　As we return to our unity with you,
　　　　live in us
　　　　　　that we may be signs of your grace.
　　As we embark on this Lenten journey,
　　　　walk with us and teach us
　　　　　　the wisdom of your love.
　　With joyous hope, we pray. Amen.

SENDING FORTH

Benediction (Joel 2, Psalm 51)
　　Trust in God's mercy.
　　Live in God's love.
　　Believe in God's grace.
　　Rejoice in God's name!

CONTEMPORARY OPTIONS

Contemporary Gathering Words (2 Corinthians 5–6)
　　Ashes to ashes, dust to dust.
　　This is an evening of darkness and despair.

But wait!
Christ calls to us with promises of hope.
Christ calls with words of love.
Christ calls with a life of grace.
Out of the ashes, a phoenix flies forth.
Out of the dust, humanity is created.
Out of the tomb, Christ rises and death is no more.
Ashes to love, dust to joy.
This is the Easter promise of our Lenten journey.

Praise Sentences (Psalm 51)

Open your lips, and declare God's praise.
Praise the God of steadfast love!
Open your lips, and declare God's praise.
Praise the God of steadfast love!

Alternate Call to Worship (Psalm 51)

O God, open our lips, as we declare your praise.
Praising you, we remember your mercy.
Open our lips, as we declare your praise.
Praising you, we recall your love.
Open our lips, as we declare your praise.
Praising you, we return to your arms of grace.

FEBRUARY 10, 2008

First Sunday in Lent
Mary Petrina Boyd

COLOR
Purple

SCRIPTURE READINGS
Genesis 2:15-17; 3:1-7; Psalm 32; Romans 5:12-19; Matthew 4:1-11

THEME IDEAS
Today's scriptures address sin and temptation. The narratives of Genesis and Matthew tell of the garden of Eden and Jesus' temptation. The psalm promises God's forgiveness, and Romans declares the promise of justification and life for all. Together, the scriptures admit human sin and failure while offering forgiveness and justification. The season of Lenten repentance offers an invitation to turn back to God and find life.

INVITATION AND GATHERING

Call to Worship (Psalm 32, Romans 5)
Be glad in the Lord and rejoice, O righteous!
Shout for joy, you upright in heart!
God is a hiding place for us
and preserves us from trouble.
The Lord surrounds and protects us.

God's love is a free gift, offering life.
In God we have life and hope.
Be glad in the Lord and rejoice, O righteous!
Shout for joy, you upright in heart!

Opening Prayer (Genesis 2–3, Psalm 32)
Creating God,
give us new opportunities
to live in the fullness of your love.
Forgiving God,
deliver us from all
that keeps us from you.
Draw us close to you.
By your love,
make us a righteous people.
Teach us to shout for joy
as we rejoice in your grace. Amen.

PROCLAMATION AND RESPONSE

Prayer of Confession (Genesis 2–3, Psalm 32, Romans 5, Matthew 4)
When temptation whispers,
we want to answer that call:
we long to be powerful;
we want to be all-knowing;
we long to be in control;
we want things our own way.
Compassionate God,
give us courage to admit our failings;
teach us to speak the truth;
keep us from any deceit.
Transform our hearts by the power of your grace,
that we may accept your forgiveness,
and live with joy
the life you give us. Amen.

Words of Assurance

Happy are those whose transgression is forgiven,
    whose sin is covered.
It is Jesus Christ who brings life
    and makes us righteous.

Invitation to the Word (Psalm 32)

Open our hearts
    to hear your word of grace.
Give us honest spirits,
    that we may receive your gift.

Response to the Word/Sermon (Genesis 2–3, Psalm 32)

God of all patience,
    give us the strength to resist temptation,
    the courage to admit where we have failed,
    and the wisdom to accept your loving forgiveness.
Amen.

THANKSGIVING AND COMMUNION

Communion Liturgy (Genesis 2–3, Romans 5, Matthew 4)

It is right, and a good and joyful thing,
    always and everywhere, to give thanks to you,
    God Almighty, creator of heaven and earth.
Creator God,
    you breathed forth your love,
    and the world came into existence.
You created a home for all creatures,
    a place of abundance and life.
You placed humanity in a place of goodness,
    and gave us meaningful work to do,
    caring for your creation.
When our love failed,
    when we longed for knowledge and power,
    when we turned from you to follow others,
    your love remained steadfast.
You delivered us from our captivity

to sin and disobedience,
clothed us in garments of righteousness,
and gave us your word to guide our journey.
And so, with your people on earth,
and all the company of heaven,
we praise your name
and join in their unending hymn.
Holy, holy, holy Lord,
God of power and might,
heaven and earth are full of your glory.
Hosanna in the highest.
Blessed is the one who comes
in the name of the Lord.
Hosanna in the highest.

Holy are you and blessed is your Son, Jesus Christ.
In him, you give your free gift of grace
to all the world.
He showed us your way;
taught us how to resist evil;
showed us how to work for justice;
told us of your abundant love;
and by the free offering of himself,
delivered us from judgment and condemnation,
that we might live to your glory.
In this love, Christ gave birth to the church,
which is his body, shared for the world.
(Follow with words of institution.)

Unison Prayer (Genesis 2, Matthew 4)

God of our Lenten journey,
thank you for your presence along the way,
for your guidance when times are difficult,
and for your promise of life in Jesus Christ.
Lead us from those things that bring death to us,
those things that kill what is good,
those things that destroy your good gifts.

Open our souls to be honest with you,
    knowing that you will receive us as we are,
    and that only in you will we find forgiveness
        and a new beginning.
It is so easy to give in to the world's temptations:
    to use too much of the world's resources,
    to take advantage of other people,
    to seek power instead of service.
Help us see others as you see them,
    and serve those in need.
Grant us your wisdom,
    that we may not only pray for those in need,
    but walk with them as well,
        offering our comfort and relief. Amen.

Invitation to the Offering (Psalm 32, Romans 5)
We have received the abundant gift
    of God's forgiveness.
God has blessed us in so many ways.
Rejoicing, let us bring our gifts to God.

Offering Prayer (Genesis 2–3)
God of creation,
    all that we have
        comes from you.
We bring our gifts
    from a deep sense of thankfulness
        for all that you have done.
Use this offering
    to spread your gift of life
        to all of the world,
        that everyone might know
            the wonders of your forgiving love.
Use us as your forgiven servants,
    rejoicing in your gifts of life. Amen.

SENDING FORTH

Benediction (Psalm 32, Romans 5)

Go forth as God's forgiven people.
Turn from sin and delight in good works.
Share the love of God with the world.
Rejoice and shout for joy!

CONTEMPORARY OPTIONS

Contemporary Gathering Words (Matthew 4, Romans 5)

Come as you are to this place.
Find the blessings of God's love here.
Jesus comes not to the powerful and mighty,
    but to those who are hungry for love,
    to those who feel unworthy,
    to those who have failed.
Come; delight in God's presence.

Praise Sentences (Psalm 32, Romans 5)

Happy are those who know that God forgives them!
Be glad and rejoice!
Shout for joy!
Rejoice in the free gift of God's love!
Live in the fullness of God's grace!

FEBRUARY 17, 2008

Second Sunday in Lent
B. J. Beu

COLOR
Purple

SCRIPTURE READINGS
Genesis 12:1-4a; Psalm 121; Romans 4:1-5, 13-17; John 3:1-17

THEME IDEAS
The readings from Genesis and the Gospel of John speak of God's blessings, that we might be a blessing to others. If Abram will set out in faith, God promises to bless those who bless him, and to curse those who curse him (Genesis 12:3). And John assures us that God's Son was not sent into the world to condemn the world, but to save it (John 3:17). How can our response to God be anything less than extending that blessing to others? Psalm 121 makes it clear that the One who helps us and keeps us from evil is the same God who created the heavens and the earth.

INVITATION AND GATHERING

Call to Worship or Benediction (Genesis 12)
The God of Abram leads us forward.
Lead on, O God; lead us home.

The God of Abram is here to bless us.
Bless us, O God, that we might be a blessing.
The God of Abram leads us forward
Lead on, O God; lead us home.

Opening Prayer (John 3)
Loving God,
you delight in showing us your kingdom,
a place of blessing,
a place of light,
a place of Spirit and truth.
May we be born anew in your Spirit,
that we might see the glory
you have in store for us
and for the world.
For you sent your Son into our world,
not to condemn us or put us to shame,
but that we might have life
and have it abundantly. Amen.

PROCLAMATION AND RESPONSE

Prayer of Confession (Psalm 121, John 3, Genesis 12)
Maker of heaven and earth,
lift our eyes to the hills,
that we might find our help
in times of trial.
Forgive us when, like Nicodemus,
our vision is focused on the ground:
ignoring your call to follow you;
refusing your blessings
for fear of the obligation to bless others
whom we do not want to meet.
Even when we follow,
we often do so out of fear:
fear of your disappointment,
fear of your awesome power,
fear of your wrath.

Teach our hearts anew to trust your Spirit
and the promise of your blessings. Amen.

Words of Assurance (Genesis 12:2)
Hear the words spoken by God to Abram,
words God speaks to the church and to us
when we live as faithful followers of Christ:
"I will make of you a great nation,
and I will bless you, and make your name great,
so that you will be a blessing."

Response to the Word/Sermon (John 3, Genesis 12)
Eternal God,
your Spirit moves through us
like an ever-flowing stream.
Your word, like the wind,
blows where it chooses.
Reside in our hearts this day,
that we may be born from above
into newness of life.
Revive our spirit,
that we might be blessed
to be a blessing to others. Amen.

Call to Prayer (Psalm 121)
The One who made heaven and earth is listening.
The One who keeps your soul is here for you now.
The One who saves you from all evil
awaits your prayers of thanksgiving and petition.
Lift up your eyes to the hills,
behold the One who is your help,
and offer up your prayers to God.
(A time for silent prayer or Prayer of the People may follow.)

THANKSGIVING AND COMMUNION

Offering Prayer (Genesis 12)
Gracious God,
just as you blessed Abram

when he ventured out in faith,
   you have blessed us with so much.
Help us see our gifts and offerings,
   not as fruit of our hard work,
   but as blessings we have received from you.
We offer you these offerings
   in response to your abundant gifts and blessings.
Amen.

SENDING FORTH

Benediction (Psalm 121:5-8)

Hear the words of the psalmist:
   The LORD is your keeper.
   The LORD is your shade at your right hand.
   The sun shall not strike you by day,
      nor the moon by night.
   The LORD will keep you from all evil.
   God will keep your life.
   The LORD will keep your going out and your coming in
      from this time on and forevermore.

CONTEMPORARY OPTIONS

Contemporary Gathering Words or Benediction (Genesis 12)

Leave your well-worn paths and walk with God.
   But we are secure where we are.
Walk in new paths and you will be blessed.
   Can't God bless us on our own turf?
If you will walk in faith,
God will bless those who bless you,
and curse those who curse you.
   Lead on, O God,
   your faithful people await.
Receive God's blessing to be a blessing to others.

Praise Sentences (1 Corinthians 1, John 1)

God sent Christ to save us!
God sent Christ to free us!
God sent Christ to give us life!
Praise the Spirit, who gives us rebirth!
Praise the Spirit!
Praise the Spirit!

FEBRUARY 24, 2008

Third Sunday in Lent
Laura Jaquith Bartlett

COLOR
Purple

SCRIPTURE READINGS
Exodus 17:1-7; Psalm 95; Romans 5:1-11; John 4:5-42

THEME IDEAS
The gospel story of the Samaritan woman at the well offers many twists and turns, with enough fodder for a year of sermons. But surely one of the most compelling images of this passage is of the living water. For a world that still thirsts for spiritual renewal, today's scripture offers a beautiful vision of hope—a vision that can be seen, heard, and felt. To the ancient Israelites, to the Samaritan woman, and even to us, God offers the gift of living water.

INVITATION AND GATHERING

Call to Worship (Exodus 17, John 4)
Come, all who are thirsty!
Christ offers living water to all.
Come, all who have doubts.
Christ offers living water to all.
Come, all who long for rest.

Christ offers living water to all.
Come, all who are in need of God's love.
Christ offers living water to all.
Come and worship!

Opening Prayer (Exodus 17, John 4)
Generous God,
  we have come to you thirsty.
We are parched from the challenges
  of simply living
    in a twenty-first century world.
We deal with computer crashes,
  identity theft, and ever-higher gas prices.
But we also know the ageless sins
  of poverty, war, and abuse.
Guide us back to your well, O God.
Open our eyes;
  strengthen our faith;
  nourish our souls.
You alone offer the living water
  that sustains us.
Quench our thirst
  with the Love that is you. Amen.

PROCLAMATION AND RESPONSE

Prayer of Confession (Exodus 17, John 4)
God of the ages,
  you know us better than we know ourselves.
You already know our history,
  our shortcomings, our failings.
And yet you also know of our great need.
You alone know the depth of our thirst.
Even when we are too ashamed to admit our need,
  you offer the sustenance of your love.
We pray to you, God of mercy,
  that you might shower us
    with the living water

that refreshes our souls.
Quench our thirst.
Restore our faith.
And let us be washed clean
   in the river of your forgiveness.
(During a time of quiet reflection before the Words of Assurance, you might turn on a tabletop fountain or play a sound clip of a fountain or river.)

Words of Assurance (John 4)

Jesus said,
   "Those who drink of the water that I will give them
      will never be thirsty.
   The water that I will give
      will become in them a spring of water
         gushing up to eternal life."
Through Jesus Christ,
   God has showered us
      with the blessing of living water.
Let us rejoice in the cleansing river
   of God's forgiving love!

Passing the Peace of Christ

Splash and rejoice in the river of God's love.
There is water enough for everyone!

Response to the Word/Sermon (John 4)

The living water of God's love
   gushes out in a river
      that is abundant enough for everyone:
         enough for Samaritan women;
         enough for confused disciples;
         enough for anxious teenagers;
         enough for overworked teachers;
         enough for lonely widows;
         enough for stressed-out professionals;
         enough for homeless alcoholics;
         enough for single parents;
         enough for me.

The living water of God's love
   gushes out in a river
      that is abundant enough for everyone.

THANKSGIVING AND COMMUNION

Prayers of the People (Exodus 17, John 4)
(Following each prayer petition, use this response.)
O God, we are thirsty.
Send us your Living Water.

Offering Prayer (John 4)
God of abundance,
   your gifts gush over us
      in a stream of love.
We who have drunk deeply of your living water
   offer our gifts to you.
Take our lives, O Lord.
Empower us to step into the river
   and flow through the world,
      offering the gift of your love
         to others who thirst still.
We pray and serve in the name of Christ. Amen.

SENDING FORTH

Benediction (John 4)
Go out and join the river of God's love.
Go out and carry Christ's living water to the world.
Go out and be sustained and nurtured
   by the abundant grace of the Holy Spirit.
Go out to a thirsty world
   and offer the spring of water
      gushing up to eternal life. Amen.

CONTEMPORARY OPTIONS

Contemporary Gathering Words (John 4)
Come to the water, where your thirst will be quenched.
Come to the love, where your pain will be comforted.

Come to the light, where we worship in truth.
Come to Christ, the deep well, with water enough for all.
Come!

Praise Sentences (John 4)

Christ offers us living water.
When we drink this water,
    we will never thirst again.
The living water of Christ will become in us
    a spring of water, gushing up to eternal life.
Come drink of the Living Water!

MARCH 2, 2008

Fourth Sunday in Lent
One Great Hour of Sharing
Mary J. Scifres

COLOR
Purple

SCRIPTURE READINGS
1 Samuel 16:1-13; Psalm 23; Ephesians 5:8-14; John 9:1-41

THEME IDEAS
Seeing with the eyes of Christ is a perspective for which most people yearn. Today's scriptures reveal many examples of such vision. Samuel learns to see differently as he seeks to anoint the new king of Israel. The psalmist learns to see with faith and trust, even in the darkest valleys. The Ephesians are called to walk in the light of Christ, rather than following the world's guidance. And in John's Gospel, a blind man is the only one who can truly see who Jesus is. We too can see rightly if we listen for God's guidance and view the world with the light of Christ's presence in our lives.

INVITATION AND GATHERING

Call to Worship (Ephesians 5)
Come; walk in the light!
God will show us the way.
Come; worship our God.

The Spirit has called us here.
Come; listen and learn of God's love.
The love of Christ Jesus is ours!

Opening Prayer (Psalm 23, Ephesians 5)
Shepherding God,
guide us on this Lenten journey.
Reveal your pathways of love and righteousness,
that we may walk as your children of light.
Help us see your vision for the world,
that we may work as your disciples
and live as your people.
In Christ's name we pray. Amen.

Proclamation and Response

Prayer of Confession (John 9)
God of amazing grace,
forgive our blind spots
that keep us from seeing you;
forgive our blind spots
that keep us from seeing others
as you see them;
forgive our avoidance of your healing touch
and your revealing spirit.
Touch us with your healing hands of love.
Help us sing of your amazing grace,
knowing that we who once were blind
can now truly see.
Help us know your amazing grace,
trusting that we who once were lost
are now forever found by your love.
In the name of your gracious love, we pray.

Words of Assurance (John 9)
Trust, my friends, that amazing grace is ours.
We may have been blind.
But now we can see!
We may have been lost.
But in Christ we are found!

Open your eyes.
Christ is here.
God's love is ours!

Prayer of Preparation (John 9)

God of light and life,
    open our eyes and our hearts.
Open our ears and our minds.
Open our lives to your ways.
May our vision be your vision.
Where we are blind and stubborn,
    wash away these obstacles,
      that we may follow in your footsteps
        and walk in your ways. Amen.

Response to the Word/Sermon (1 Samuel 16, John 9)

With vision and hope,
the ancients followed God.
    With vision and hope,
    we continue their journey.
With faith and joy,
our ancestors proclaimed Jesus as the Christ.
    With faith and joy,
    we proclaim and praise Christ's name.
In light and love,
disciples became ministers of God.
    In light and love,
    we too become disciples in ministry.

(Optional Litany ending, if used as Call to Worship)
Let us worship in the spirit and truth
of Christ's love.

THANKSGIVING AND COMMUNION

Offering Prayer (Ephesians 5, John 9)

We thank you, O God of light,
    for guiding us out of darkness
      and into life.

We praise you for your healing touch
  as you repair the damaged parts of our lives.
We offer these gifts in gratitude and praise.
Through these gifts,
  create points of light and places of healing.
In the name of the Great Physician, we pray. Amen.

SENDING FORTH

Benediction (Ephesians 5)

In the Lord, we are light!
In Christ Jesus, we are love!
Let us live as children of light!
May our fruits be goodness and truth!

(Or)

Benediction (Ephesians 5, John 9)

We who have seen Jesus have a vision to share.
May we live that vision each day.
We who know God have a message to bring.
May we proclaim that message aloud.

CONTEMPORARY OPTIONS

Contemporary Gathering Words (Ephesians 5)

Wake up! The Son is shining!
Wake up! The Son is shining!
Wake up! Christ's love is upon us!
Wake up! Christ's love is here!

Praise Sentences (John 9)

Jesus is the light of the world!
Jesus is the light of our lives!
Jesus is the light of the world!
Jesus is the light of our lives!

MARCH 9, 2008

Fifth Sunday in Lent
Jamie D. Greening

COLOR
Purple

SCRIPTURE READINGS
Ezekiel 37:1-14; Psalm 130; Romans 8:6-11; John 11:1-45

THEME IDEAS
Out of death comes life. Ezekiel prophesies to dry bones in the valley of death, and life springs forth before his very eyes. John records Jesus' bold statement, "Those who believe in me, even though they die, will live" (John 11:25), which sets the stage for his command: "Lazarus, come out!" Paul echoes the paradox of life from death, reminding us that the flesh is death but the Spirit is life. The psalmist reflects on the long death of nightfall while waiting for the morning's resurrection miracle of sunrise.

INVITATION AND GATHERING

Call to Worship (Psalm 130)
Out of the depths of our sins, we cry to you.
Come and redeem us.
Open your ears and hear our voices.
Come and redeem us.
With reverence, we await forgiveness.

Come and redeem us.
We watch for your Word, and hope in your love.
Come and redeem us.

Opening Prayer (Ezekiel 37)
Almighty God,
  we have gathered as dry bones
    in our Lenten season,
    longing for your refreshing words.
Lord Jesus,
  let the sinew of your presence
    be real in our hearts and minds.
Holy Spirit,
  invigorate us with life
    and give us breath to worship you.
In the power of the Triune God, amen.

PROCLAMATION AND RESPONSE

Prayer of Confession (Romans 8)
In your mercy, Mighty God,
  we ask that you forgive us
    for setting our mind on the flesh:
      for the sin of greed;
    (Pause for silence.)
      for the sin of lust;
    (Pause for silence.)
      for the sin of neglect;
    (Pause for silence.)
      for the sin of anger;
    (Pause for silence.)
      for the sin of addiction;
    (Pause for silence.)
      for the sin of oppression;
    (Pause for silence.)
      for the sin of intolerance;
    (Pause for silence.)
      for the sin of hate;

(Pause for silence.)
Jesus, free us from our sins,
>that we might live in your Spirit.

Words of Assurance (Psalm 130)
Women, men, and children,
>beloved of God,
>>rejoice that God hears our prayers.

If our failings and faults were held against us,
>none could stand.
But with God there is forgiveness,
>and this gives us hope.
Through Christ Jesus our sins are forgiven.

Response to the Word/Sermon (John 11)
As Lazarus in the tomb
>heard your words of power,
>>so have we.
On this day,
>grant us the power
>>to stand up on renewed legs of faith.
May we walk out of darkness
>and into the light of righteousness.
May the ministry of God's word
>remove our grave clothes
>>and embrace us in the kingdom of God.

THANKSGIVING AND COMMUNION

Call to Prayer (Psalm 130, John 11)
Though we are engulfed by our needs,
>the Lord hears our prayers.
God is listening.
God weeps when we hurt,
>and yet has the power to redeem
>>and bring life to any situation.
Offer your prayers
>and watch for the morning of renewed hope.

Offering Prayer (Ezekiel 37, Psalm 130, Romans 8, John 11)
Great Triune God,
    you give us the best gift—
        the gift of life.
We bring our gifts to you.
Though they are but cold silver and gold,
    mute money of paper and ink,
    you use our humble gifts
        to bring life to your people
            both here and far away.
Bring a new day of generosity
    and sharing in our world. Amen.

SENDING FORTH

Benediction (Ezekiel 37, Psalm 130, Romans 8, John 11)
In the valley of dry bones, remember:
God's words are life.
In the tomb of despair, listen:
God's words are life.
As we leave this place, remember:
God's words are life.
God's words are life.

CONTEMPORARY OPTIONS

Contemporary Gathering Words (Ezekiel 37, John 11)
Do you feel dead today?
No one has to live that way.
Is your spirit dry?
It is enough to make Jesus cry.
Gather; hear; live anew.
God's Word is here for you.
Lift your heart; raise your head.
Jesus gives life to the dead.

Praise Sentences (Romans 8)

Christ's presence is here with us.
The Spirit of God dwells within.
We belong to God.

MARCH 16, 2008

Palm/Passion Sunday
B. J. Beu

COLOR
Purple

PALM SUNDAY READINGS
Psalm 118:1-2, 19-29; Matthew 21:1-11

PASSION SUNDAY READINGS
Isaiah 50:4-9a; Psalm 31:9-16; Philippians 2:5-11; Matthew 26:14–27:66

THEME IDEAS (PALM SUNDAY)
Palm Sunday presents worship planners with a quandary: to focus the entire service on Jesus' triumphal entry into Jerusalem, and risk moving from the joy of Palm Sunday to the joy of Easter without moving through the anguish of Holy Thursday and Good Friday; or to move quickly from the parade atmosphere of Palm Sunday into the turning of the crowds, the betrayal, and the passion narratives, and thereby risk losing attendance at the forthcoming Holy Week services. Since Easter makes no sense without Christ's passion and death, we will err on the side of including the passion events in today's service. Fickleness of heart and betrayal are themes in this day's service.

INVITATION AND GATHERING

Call to Worship (Psalm 118)

This is the day that the Lord has made.
Let us rejoice and be glad in it.
Blessed is the one who comes in the name of the Lord.
God's steadfast love endures forever.
The stone that the builders rejected
has become the chief cornerstone.
This is the Lord's doing.
It is marvelous in our eyes.
Bind the festival procession with branches.
Jesus is the gate of the Lord.
The righteous enter through him.
This is the day that the Lord has made.
Let us rejoice and be glad in it.

Opening Prayer (Matthew 21; Philippians 2)

Blessed One,
    you entered Jerusalem in lowly estate,
        riding on a donkey;
    you emptied yourself,
        forsaking the power to command,
            and came as a servant to all.
Son of David,
    come to us now and be our King,
        that we too may sing our hosannas!
Amen.

PROCLAMATION AND RESPONSE

Prayer of Confession (Matthew 26–27)

God of righteousness,
    we would rather sing hosannas with a cheering crowd,
    than stand up for our convictions
        in the face of an angry mob;
    we would rather dine with you at your table,
        than stand up for you in a courtyard of accusers;

we would rather fancy ourselves as your champions,
    than admit to ourselves
        how easily we could betray you with a kiss.
Forgive our fickle faith.
Heal our hesitant hearts.
And deepen our irresolute discipleship. Amen.

Words of Assurance (Psalm 118)
God has opened the gates of righteousness,
    and the righteous enter through it.
The One who is our cornerstone,
    the One the builders rejected,
    has become our salvation,
    offering us forgiveness
        and fullness of grace.
Amen and amen.

Response to the Word/Sermon (1 Peter 2)
Merciful God,
    we tremble when we think how easily
        Judas betrayed you;
    we shake when we realize how many times
        like Peter, we have denied you,
        through our actions.
May your words live within us and strengthen us,
    that we might keep our eyes focused on the cross
        and walk with you to the end. Amen.

Call to Prayer (Psalm 31)
Like broken vessels,
    we need your healing, O God.
Like those who are dead,
    we need the stirring of new life within us.
Like an army surrounded by its enemies,
    we need your deliverance.
Let us lift up our prayers to God,
    the One who delivers us from evil,
    the One whose steadfast love
        makes us whole again.

THANKSGIVING AND COMMUNION

Offering Prayer (Genesis 12)
Holy One,
your love for us is so great
that you gave us your own Son
to teach us the ways of life and death.
May the gifts and offerings we bring this morning
reflect our gratitude:
for Christ's gift of self,
for Christ's anguish and passion,
for Christ's never-failing love. Amen.

SENDING FORTH

Benediction (Psalm 118)
The gates of righteousness are thrown wide.
Christ has blessed us with life.
The path of salvation is made plain.
Christ has blessed us with truth.
The cornerstone of our faith is sure.
Christ has blessed us with grace.
The gates of righteousness are thrown wide.

CONTEMPORARY OPTIONS

Contemporary Gathering Words (Psalm 118)
What's up with the builders?
They have rejected the rock of our faith.
What's up with God?
God has made this rock the chief cornerstone.
What's up with us?
We give thanks that God is our builder,
that Christ is the rock of our faith.
Come; let us worship.

Praise Sentences (Psalm 118)
Give thanks to the Lord,
for God is good.

Give thanks to the Lord,
 for God's steadfast love endures forever.
Give thanks to the Lord,
 for God is good.
God is good indeed!

MARCH 20, 2008

Holy Thursday
Mary J. Scifres

COLOR

Purple

SCRIPTURE READINGS

Exodus 12:1-4 (5-10) 11-14; Psalm 116:1-4, 12-19; 1 Corinthians 11:23-26; John 13:1-17, 31b-35

THEME IDEAS

So many themes can arise on this night: servanthood, forgiveness, grace, sacrifice, bread and communion. But each of these themes carries an underlying theme that is such a crucial part of the human journey: the theme of second chances. The Egyptians are given yet one more chance to release the Hebrew people, and yet they do not. The Hebrew people are given the chance to proclaim their role as God's people by marking their doorpost and being passed over when death comes to Egypt. The psalmist sings of escape and release from bondage; and John recounts Jesus giving the disciples one more chance to understand the concept of humble servanthood. Indeed, Holy Thursday can be a time of second chances. This is our Holy Week, a time to proclaim our role as Christ's people as we remember Jesus' great love and many sacrifices. This is our Holy Week, a time to put to death the sins and mistakes of our past and prepare

to rise anew, forgiven and reconciled, on Easter Sunday.
Let this time of second chances breathe new life into our
spiritual journeys.

INVITATION AND GATHERING

Call to Worship (1 Corinthians 11, John 13)
Tonight we will eat the bread of life
and drink the wine of forgiveness.
We will taste the promise of grace.
We will sing spiritual songs and remember stories of old.
We will embrace the truth of Christ's love.
Let us worship in remembrance and praise.

Opening Prayer (1 Corinthians 11, John 13)
Servant God,
we come with humble hearts
upon bowed knees.
We are amazed at your servant spirit
that cares for us and upholds us.
Be with us this evening
as we remember your Passover meal
shared with your disciples.
Be with us in the breaking of the bread,
in the sharing of the cup,
in the washing of feet,
in the praying of prayers,
in the very act of remembering.
Fill us with your humble spirit
that we may serve others as abundantly
as we are served by you.
In Christ's name, we pray. Amen.

(Or)

Opening Prayer (1 Corinthians 11, John 13)
God of second chances and new beginnings,
let this Holy Week be a time of preparation.
Open our hearts and minds

to your grace and guidance.
Embrace us with your love,
> that we may remember with gratitude
>> the forgiveness you have offered us
>>> time and time again.
Envelop us with your grace,
> that we may accept this opportunity
>> to rise again with Christ,
>>> and move forward into new beginnings.
Fill us with your Spirit,
> that we may live
>> as your servants in the world. Amen.

PROCLAMATION AND RESPONSE

Prayer of Confession (John 13)
Gracious God,
> we pray for forgiveness on this holy night.
Where we have not served,
> fill us with your servant spirit.
Where we have not loved,
> transform us with your loving ways.
Where we have not forgiven,
> grace us with your forgiving nature.
Where we have rejected your offer of second chances,
> give us yet one more chance.
Lift us up and guide us forward
> into opportunities of grace and love.
In Christ's name, we pray. Amen.

Words of Assurance
In the name of Jesus Christ, you are forgiven!
In the name of Jesus Christ, we are all forgiven!

THANKSGIVING AND COMMUNION

Call to Communion (1 Corinthians 11, John 13)
As often as we gather,
> **we gather in remembrance of Christ.**
When we care for another in need,

we care for Christ our Lord.
When we break the bread and share the cup,
we participate in the kingdom of God.
Come, all things are ready.

Communion Prayer (1 Corinthians 11, John 13)

Servant God,
    we remember this night
        your many gifts of grace and servanthood
           as you walked upon this earth;
    we remember this night
        your many gifts of grace and servanthood
           as you touch our lives today.
With humility and gratitude,
    we come to the table
        and accept your gracious gifts
           of forgiveness and love.
Christ Jesus,
    we remember that night
        when you took a loaf of bread,
        gave thanks, broke it, saying,
           "This is my body that is for you.
           Do this in remembrance of me."
We remember that in the same way,
    you took the cup and said,
        "This cup is the new covenant in my blood.
        Do this, as often as you drink it,
           in remembrance of me."
We remember on this night
    why we eat this bread and drink this cup:
        to proclaim the great mystery of faith:
    Christ has died. Christ is risen.
    Christ will come again.

Pour out your Holy Spirit on all those gathered here,
    that we might be disciples of your new covenant
        of love and grace.
Pour out your Holy Spirit
    on these gifts of bread and wine,

that they may be for us
    the life and love of Christ,
that we may be for the world
    the body of Christ,
        redeemed by your gracious love.
By your Spirit,
    make us one with Christ,
    one with each other,
        and one in ministry to all the world.
In Christ's name we pray. Amen.

SENDING FORTH

Benediction (1 Corinthians 11, John 13)
    Go forth with hope for new beginnings.
    Remembering the past,
    we move into the future.
    Go forth with trust in God's grace.
    Remembering Christ's love,
    we go as disciples of love.

CONTEMPORARY OPTIONS

Contemporary Gathering Words or Invitation to
Communion (John 13, Psalm 116)
    Come to the festival of love.
    Come with thanksgiving and praise.
    Come to the festival of grace.
    Come with thanksgiving and praise.
    Come to the festival of life.
    Come with thanksgiving and praise.

Praise Sentences (Psalm 116)
    Love the Lord who hears!
    Love the Lord who saves!
    Love our God who gives!
    Love our God who loves!

MARCH 21, 2008

Good Friday
A Service of Tenebrae
B. J. Beu

COLOR
Black or None

GOOD FRIDAY SCRIPTURE READINGS
Isaiah 52:13–53:12; Psalm 22; Hebrews 10:16-25; John 18:1–19:42

TENEBRAE READINGS
Although a traditional Service of Tenebrae contains sixteen readings taken from John 18:1–19:42, this service contains fourteen readings culled from all four Gospels. Just as no Christmas Eve nativity would be complete without the arrival of the Magi, no passion account is complete without elements omitted from John's narrative. The readings conclude at Jesus' death, at the climax of the passion narrative, and omit the two burial readings: John 19:31-37 and 19:38-42.

THEME IDEAS
Suffering, rejection, and loss focus our readings. Although Isaiah 52 begins with the inevitable exaltation of God's servant, it is a chilling reminder of how easily we turn on God's chosen ones. A Service of Tenebrae, or

"darkness" is an extended meditation on Christ's passion. Psalm 22, which Jesus quotes while hanging on the cross, conveys the feeling of being abandoned by God when the forces of destruction hold sway. Peter's betrayal of his friend and teacher in the courtyard depicts how low we can sink, despite our love and convictions.

INVITATION AND GATHERING

Call to Worship

Were you there when they crucified my Lord?
We were the silence when no bird sang.
Were you in the garden when the disciples fell asleep?
We were the betrayal in Judas's kiss.
Were you in the courtyard when the cock crowed
three times?
We were the denial in Peter's mouth.
Were you among the scoffers when Jesus was flogged?
We were the whip in the soldier's hand.
Were you in Pilate's chamber when he washed his hands
of Jesus' sentence?
We were the hatred of the crowd;
the indifference in Pilate's heart.
Were you there when the soldiers dressed Jesus as a king?
We were the mockery in the crown of thorns.
Were you among the onlookers at Golgotha?
We were the nails that pierced Jesus' hands
and feet.
Were you there when they crucified my Lord?
We were the silence when no bird sang.

Opening Prayer (Isaiah 52–53, Psalm 22)

Elusive One,
    where do you go
        when all hope fades away?
We cry out with the psalmist,
    "My God, my God,
        why have you forsaken me?"

In hope mixed with despair,
  we strain to see you
    charging to our rescue.
Instead, we face the emptiness
  of your absence.
Your ways are beyond us, O God,
  shrouding us in mystery.
Be with us in our hour of need,
  and do not abandon us
    when we deny you.

PROCLAMATION AND RESPONSE

<u>*First Reading (Luke 22:39-53)*</u>
  (The first candle is extinguished.)

<u>*Second Reading (John 18:12-14)*</u>
  (The second candle is extinguished.)

<u>*Third Reading (Luke 22:54b-62)*</u>
  (The third candle is extinguished.)

<u>*Litany (John 18)*</u>
  There is no warmth in the fire.
  Our blood runs cold as the night.
  The one we love is in peril.
  Our courage blows away like the wind.
  Strangers recognize our fellowship with Jesus.
  Our denial pierces the soul
  like the cock's crow pierces the dawn.
  There is no warmth in the fire.
  Our tears flow cold as the night.

<u>*Fourth Reading (John 18:19-23)*</u>
  (The fourth candle is extinguished.)

<u>*Fifth Reading (Matthew 27:1-2)*</u>
  (The fifth candle is extinguished.)

<u>*Sixth Reading (Matthew 27:3-10)*</u>
  (The sixth candle is extinguished.)

Litany (Matthew 27)

Jesus stands condemned.
Stop this madness.
It is too late.
We repent of our sin.
You have been well paid.
We don't want your blood money.
It is yours all the same.
Stop this madness.
It is too late.

Seventh Reading (John 18:33-38)

(The seventh candle is extinguished.)

Eighth Reading (Matthew 27:15-24)

(The eighth candle is extinguished.)

Prayer of Confession (Matthew 27)

O Holy Mystery,
it is easier to wash our hands of responsibility
than it is to stand up for what we believe;
it is easier to defer to the judgments of others
than it is to take a principled stand.
Forgive us when we take the easy way out,
and fill us with courage
to follow the One who suffered on our behalf.
Amen.

Ninth Reading (Matthew 27:26-31)

(The ninth candle is extinguished.)

Tenth Reading (Matthew 27:32-37; John 19:20b-21)

(The tenth candle is extinguished.)

Eleventh Reading (Luke 23:35, 39-43)

(The eleventh candle is extinguished.)

Litany

Come to the cross and feel the weight of the world.
We bring the weight of our sins.
Come to the cross and feel the weight of the world.

We bring the weight of our desertions and betrayals.
Come to the cross and feel the weight of the world.
We bring the weight of our accusations and scorns.
Come to the cross and feel the weight of the world.
We bring the weight of our lives.

<u>*Twelfth Reading (Mark 15:33-34)*</u>
(The twelfth candle is extinguished.)

<u>*Thirteenth Reading (Mark 15:35-36)*</u>
(The thirteenth candle is extinguished.)

<u>*Fourteenth Reading (Matthew 27:50-51)*</u>
(As the description of the earthquake is read, a loud noise is made by a cymbal or other instrument; then the fourteenth candle is extinguished.)

SENDING FORTH

(Drape the cross with black cloth and extinguish the Christ candle. The people depart in silence. If your congregation has a gold or brass cross on its Lord's Table, try substituting a roughhewn cross with horseshoe nails.)

MARCH 23, 2008

Easter
Robert Blezard

COLOR
White

SCRIPTURE READINGS
Acts 10:34-43; Psalm 118:1-2, 14-24; Colossians 3:1-4; John 20:1-18

THEME IDEAS
The lections underscore the continuity of God's love and salvific work, reaching their conclusion in the death and resurrection of Jesus Christ. The only Hebrew Scripture offering, Psalm 118:1-2, proclaims that God's steadfast love endures forever, and then hints of the coming Christ in verse 22: "The stone that the builders rejected / has become the chief cornerstone." In describing the messiah, Acts 10:43 asserts that all the prophets testify about the saving work of Jesus. The brief passage from Colossians speaks about our death and life in Christ. Together these verses provide a firm theological foundation for the resurrection story from John 20:1-18.

INVITATION AND GATHERING

Call to Worship (Psalm 118, John 20)

The tomb is empty; Jesus is not here!
Christ is risen from the grave!
We shall not die, but live.
Let us raise glad songs of victory!
This day God has brought life from death,
and opened the gates of righteousness.
Let us enter God's gates with thanksgiving!

Opening Prayer (Colossians 3)

Holy, eternal, creator God,
through your Christ we are redeemed,
by your Spirit we are refreshed.
Help us seek the things that are above,
where Christ our risen Lord is seated with you.
Wrest our minds from things that are on earth,
and set our minds on things that are above.
Draw close and reveal our Christ,
in whom you reveal our lives.

PROCLAMATION AND RESPONSE

Prayer of Confession (Acts 10, Psalm 118)

God of mercy, God of hope,
our only source of strength and salvation,
we have ignored your commands,
forgotten your ways,
mistreated your creation.
Deserving your punishment,
we rejoice in your mercy.

Words of Assurance (Acts 10)

Good news, brothers and sisters:
God shows no partiality,
but looks with acceptance
upon all who fear God
and do what is right.

Through love and mercy,
   God sent Christ as judge
      of the living and the dead.
All who believe in Christ
   receive forgiveness of sins
      through his holy name.

Response to the Word/Sermon (John 20)
Most holy and eternal God,
   you come to us
      not because of what we are,
      but rather who we are:
         your needy children.
Faced with the mystery of your presence,
   may we not turn away in confusion,
   but linger, wait for you, and hear your voice.
With Mary Magdalene,
   may we proclaim with joy,
      "I have seen the Lord!"

THANKSGIVING AND COMMUNION

Call to Prayer (Acts 10, Psalm 118)
Let us call upon the risen One,
   of whom the prophets testify;
   whose steadfast love endures forever;
   who is our might and our salvation.

Offering Prayer (Colossians 3)
Baptized, we have died with Christ,
   and with Christ, we have been raised.
Reveal, O God, your Christ in glory,
   and reveal to us our lives in Christ.
Strengthen us to walk your paths,
   and set our minds on things above.

SENDING FORTH

Benediction (Acts 10, Psalm 118)

Christ is risen! Go forth in joy!
Preach to all people everywhere!
Testify of Jesus, the anointed one
    who forgives sins and reconciles us to God.
This is the Lord's marvelous doing.
Let us rejoice and be glad in it.

CONTEMPORARY OPTIONS

Contemporary Gathering Words (John 20, Colossians 3)

Have you seen the Lord?
Christ is risen!
Have you seen the Lord?
He is risen from the grave!
Have you seen the Lord?
We rise with Christ.
Have you seen the Lord?
We have seen the Lord!
Have you seen the Lord?
Christ is risen!

Praise Sentences

Jesus Christ is Lord of all!
Jesus Christ makes us whole.
Jesus Christ gives us peace!
Jesus Christ is Lord of all!

MARCH 30, 2008

Second Sunday of Easter
Rebecca J. Kruger Gaudino

COLOR
White

SCRIPTURE READINGS
Acts 2:14a, 22-32; Psalm 16; 1 Peter 1:3-9; John 20:19-31

THEME IDEAS
To those who have not seen the risen Christ, the three New Testament readings repeat the bold good news of Easter—that death could not hold Jesus in its power. Like Thomas and the other disciples, and like the readers of 1 Peter, however, we live in the midst of trials and suffering, doubt and fear. Jesus' resurrection invites us to a resilient, specially blessed faith (John 20:29b) that does not end with doubt or fear or suffering. Our readings proclaim that life is our ultimate end and God's aim for us, and we may rejoice even now in this "living hope" (1 Peter 1:3).

INVITATION AND GATHERING

Call to Worship (Acts 2, Psalm 16)
My heart is glad!
My soul rejoices, and my body rests secure!
For you do not abandon me.
You give me counsel.

You are at my right hand.
You show me the path of life.
Your presence is sheer joy.
You are my God; apart from you, I have no good.
Blessed is your name!

Opening Prayer (Acts 2, 1 Peter 1, John 20)
Stand among us once again, risen Christ,
and bless us with your greeting:
"Peace be with you."
Stand among us once again, Exalted Brother,
and breathe upon us your promised Spirit.
Stand among us once again,
You Who Have Escaped Death,
and give us new birth
into your living hope. Amen.

PROCLAMATION AND RESPONSE

Unison Prayer (Acts 2, Psalm 16, John 20)
Jesus, Savior, Resurrected Messiah,
we come before you from different paths:
some of us certain
of your joyful presence in our lives,
some of us not so certain
of the hope of being touched by your joy.
Yet we are all here,
reaching out to you:
for understanding,
for hope,
for joy,
for all that is imperishable.
Meet us here, today,
in all your power and consolation. Amen.

Invitation to the Word (John 20)
God of sacred texts,
speak powerfully to us today

through what is written in your holy scripture.
Help us hear the witnesses
　　to Jesus the Messiah, the Son of God,
　　and to the promises of life in his name.

THANKSGIVING AND COMMUNION

Call to Prayer (1 Peter 1, John 20)

If we are the disciples, locked in a room of fear,
　　Jesus appears to us.
If we are Thomas, full of doubt,
　　Jesus turns to us.
If we bear trials and suffering,
　　God comes to us in power.
If we rejoice,
　　we do so in the presence of God.
So let us come, whoever we are,
　　to the God of hope and life.

Invitation to the Offering (1 Peter 1)

May we give out of the love
　　that we have for Jesus Christ,
　　so that others may share
　　　　in our imperishable and unfading inheritance
　　　　of hope and life.

Offering Prayer (1 Peter 1)

God of great mercy,
　　accept our offerings,
　　given out of what is more precious than gold—
　　　　our faith in you, giver of hope and life.
And through these gifts,
　　reveal the risen Christ
　　　　in acts of mercy, love, and joy. Amen.

SENDING FORTH

Benediction (Psalm 16, 1 Peter 1, John 20)

In great mercy, God has given us a new birth
　　into a living hope,

for it is the risen Christ
who stands in our midst and says,
"Peace be with you!"
We go forth to walk the path of new life
and living hope.
And may the peace of the risen Christ be with us!

CONTEMPORARY OPTIONS

Contemporary Gathering Words (Acts 2, Psalm 16, 1 Peter 1, John 20)

We come as we are:
doubting Thomases, fearful disciples,
sorrowing exiles, rejoicing psalmists!
You come as you are:
Risen Christ, Christ of peace,
Holy Spirit, Spirit of forgiveness,
God of life, God of new birth!
Show us the fullness of your joy!
Show us the path of life and living hope!

Praise Sentences (Acts 2, Psalm 16)

You show me the ways of life.
Your presence fills me full of gladness.
My heart is glad, my soul rejoices,
and my flesh will live in hope!

APRIL 6, 2008

Third Sunday of Easter
Mary J. Scifres

COLOR
White

SCRIPTURE READINGS
Acts 2:14a, 36-41; Psalm 116:1-4, 12-19; 1 Peter 1:17-23;
Luke 24:13-35

THEME IDEAS
Opening our eyes to see Christ in our midst is a challenging step on the Christian journey, but this is the step
that leads two disciples to recognize the risen Christ.
However, opening one's eyes is only a step; for after their
experience, the disciples made known all that had hap-
pened to them. To see and to tell are the themes of this
Sunday in the Easter season.

INVITATION AND GATHERING
Call to Worship (Luke 24)
Open your eyes!
  Christ is here!
Open your ears!
  God is still speaking!
Open your hearts!
  The Spirit is moving!
Open the doors, for worship has begun!

Opening Prayer (Luke 24)

Risen Lord,
    speak to our hearts this day.
Burn your message of life and hope
    onto our very souls,
    that we might hear your voice
        and know your promise.
Stay with us in this time of worship.
Reveal your word,
    and feed us with your wisdom.

PROCLAMATION AND RESPONSE

Prayer of Confession (Luke 24)

God of Easter hope,
    grant us the courage
        to believe in your resurrection miracles.
Forgive us when we fall into despair or blindness.
Give us new eyes
    to truly see you walking with us,
    standing beside us,
    living in our neighborhoods,
    and speaking through our friends
        and our enemies.
Forgive us when we prefer simple answers
    to prophetic challenges.
Forgive us when we cling to old, familiar ways,
    and refuse to see the extraordinary miracles
        you set before us.
Open our eyes,
    that we might see you
        standing before us
            in your resurrected glory,
    proclaiming the miracle of life and love
        that never ends.

Words of Assurance (1 Peter 1)

Speaking the truth to ourselves in love,
    we cleanse our souls.

In Christ Jesus,
>we have been born anew,
>>through the everlasting, living word of God.

My friends, in Christ Jesus,
>we are raised up from the dead places of sin
>>and brought forth into the light of new life.

Rise with Christ,
>for we are born anew in God's love!

Prayer of Preparation (Luke 24)

Risen Lord,
>speak to our hearts through your word.

Open our ears
>to hear the resurrection story anew.

Reveal your purposes and promises in us,
>that we may go forth
>>and live as your disciples in the world.

THANKSGIVING AND COMMUNION

Invitation to the Offering (Psalm 116)

What shall we return to Christ
>for God's many gifts?

With the name of Christ Jesus on our lips,
>let us sing God's praises
>>and offer words of thanksgiving.

In gratitude and praise,
>let us give of ourselves and our time
>>as an offering to God.

Offering Prayer (Psalm 116, Luke 24)

Loving God,
>we offer these gifts of thanksgiving and praise
>>as tokens of our gratitude
>>>for all that you do
>>>>and all that you are in our lives.

For raising us up to new life,
>we praise you.

For revealing your word in our lives,
    we are ever grateful.
For living within us,
    we thank you.
May our words and our actions
    be a glory and an honor to you,
    Risen Christ, Living God, Spirit of Life.
Amen and Amen.

The Great Thanksgiving (An Act of Preparation for Holy Communion)

The Lord be with you.
And also with you.
Lift up your hearts.
We lift them up to the Lord.
Let us give thanks to the Lord our God.
It is right to give our thanks and praise.

It is right, and a good and joyful thing,
    always and everywhere to give thanks to you,
    Almighty God, creator of heaven and earth.
In ancient days, you created us in your image,
    and invited us to be reflections of your glory.
When we fell short and dimmed the brilliance
    of your light shining through us,
    you held our hands and walked with us
      out of the garden and into all the corners of the earth.
When we were afraid to look upon your glory,
    you came as a quiet traveler, as a burning bush,
    and as a pillar of light.
You called us to be your people
    and invited us to walk in your ways.
Even when we turned away,
    you continued to walk with us
    and extended the hand of your steadfast love.
In the words of the prophets,
    you offered your wisdom and your truth.

And in the fullness of time,
    you sent your Son, Jesus Christ,
    to reveal your grace in the world.
Even when we reject and betray your ways,
    you call us into discipleship.
Even when we are blind to Christ's presence,
    you walk with us and teach us your ways.
On that journey of discipleship,
    we continue today as we come to your table
    and rejoice in your presence among us.
And so, with your people on earth,
    and all the company of heaven,
    we praise your name
    and join their unending hymn.
    Holy, holy, holy Lord, God of power and might,
        heaven and earth are full of your glory.
    Hosanna in the highest.
    Blessed is the one
        who comes in the name of the Lord.
    Hosanna in the highest.

Holy are you, and blessed is your salvation and grace,
    Jesus Christ.
When you sent Christ to this earth,
    he walked with us as brother and friend,
    and invited us to hear your truth
    and to see your ways.
Through Christ's patient love and unfailing grace,
    we are invited into your presence,
    rescued from our sins,
    and led on your path of righteousness.
With Christ's call in our lives,
    we are invited into your resurrection community,
    to proclaim your glory and to reveal the truth
    of your presence in our world.
With joy and gratitude, we break this bread
    and remember the many times

Jesus was revealed to his disciples
in the breaking of the bread.
In remembrance, we will take and eat this bread
With awe and wonder, we fill this cup
and remember the many times
when Jesus poured out his love and healing power
abundantly and lovingly.
In remembrance, we will drink from this cup
and reflect on your grace, which overflows in our lives.
And so, in remembrance of these,
your mighty acts of love and grace,
we offer ourselves in praise and thanksgiving.
As your disciples, walking with Christ,
we proclaim the mystery of faith.
Christ has died; Christ is risen;
Christ will come again.

Communion Prayer (Luke 24)

Pour out your Holy Spirit
on all of us gathered here,
that we might be your disciples in the world.
Pour out your Holy Spirit
on these gifts of bread and wine,
that we might be filled with your wisdom and truth.
By your Spirit,
may we be one with Christ,
one with each other,
and one in ministry to all the world,
until Christ comes in final victory,
and we feast at the heavenly banquet.
Through Jesus Christ,
and with the Holy Spirit in your holy church,
all honor and glory is yours, Almighty God,
now and forever more. Amen.

Giving the Bread and Cup

(The bread and wine are given to the people, with these or other
words of blessing.)

The life of Christ, revealed in you.
The love of Christ, flowing through you.

SENDING FORTH

Benediction (1 Peter 1, Luke 24)

Let mutual love continue.
**As we have loved one another with mutual love,
we go forth to share God's love with all.**
Go forth with the story of Christ on your lips,
and the love of God in your hearts.
**We go as Easter disciples, with joy and excitement,
ready to tell the great story of our salvation!**

CONTEMPORARY OPTIONS

Contemporary Gathering Words (Luke 24)

Let us walk this path together,
    that we may journey as one family upon this earth.
Let us listen for God's word to be revealed,
    even as we look for Christ to walk with us.
Let us travel with an openness of spirit,
    that the Spirit of God may enter our lives.

Praise Sentences (Psalm 116)

Love the Lord!
Lift up God's name!
Love the Lord!
Lift up God's name!

APRIL 13, 2008

Fourth Sunday of Easter
B. J. Beu

COLOR
White

SCRIPTURE READINGS
Acts 2:42-47; Psalm 23; 1 Peter 2:19-25; John 10:1-10

THEME IDEAS
The shepherd revered by the psalmist is celebrated by John as both the shepherd and the gate for the sheep. We rejoice that Jesus our shepherd calls us each by name and is the one who came that we may have abundant life (John 10:10b). This abundant life is described in Acts as a result of fellowship, breaking bread together, prayer, attention to the apostle's teachings, and sharing all things in common (Acts 2:42, 44). How far we have moved from that early paradigm of selfless giving! But when we return to our shepherd and guardian after going astray, we are healed and welcomed home (1 Peter 2:24-25).

INVITATION AND GATHERING

Call to Worship (Psalm 23, John 10)
The Lord is our Shepherd.
We are the sheep of Christ's pasture.
The Shepherd makes us lie down in green pastures.

In Christ, we dwell secure.
The Shepherd leads us beside still waters
and restores our souls.
We worship Christ, our Shepherd, our Gate.

Opening Prayer (John 10)

Loving Shepherd,
we feel the wolves close at hand.
Gather us to yourself,
that we might dwell secure in your ways.
Deliver us from evil,
that we might be free
to build a community marked by fellowship,
study, prayer, holy communion,
and sharing our possessions
according to each one's need. Amen.

PROCLAMATION AND RESPONSE

Prayer of Confession (Psalm 23, John 10)

Christ, our Shepherd, our Gate,
we would rather chart our own course,
than be shepherded like sheep;
we would rather find our own way,
than see you as the Way;
we would rather be shepherds than sheep,
who are vulnerable and exposed.
Forgive us when we bleat our resistance
as you guide us to higher pastures.
Be our Gate, our way to safe havens,
where we can dwell with you, secure. Amen.

Words of Assurance (Psalm 23)

The One who anoints our heads with oil,
the One who feeds us while our enemies look on,
the One who delivers us from evil,
invites us to dwell in the house of the Lord forever.

Response to the Word/Sermon (1 Peter 2)

Keeper of our souls,
    we were going astray like sheep,
        but now we return to you,
            our Shepherd and Guardian.
May the words we have heard
    resonate within us
        like a drum in the valley,
        and may its echo never fade. Amen.

Call to Prayer (Acts 2)

The early disciples devoted themselves to prayer,
    the teachings of the apostles,
    and sharing the bread of life.
They were a people of prayer,
    who shared their joys and concerns
    and their passions and their sorrows
        with one another and with their Lord.
For burdens shared are burdens lessened,
    and joys shared are joys enriched.
Come, let us follow their example
    and lift our prayers to God.

THANKSGIVING AND COMMUNION

Call to the Offering (Genesis 12)

Holy One,
    touch us with the awe and marvel
        that came upon those early disciples,
        as they beheld the signs and wonders
            performed in their midst
                by the apostles.
Help us have that same spirit
    and sense of community,
    sharing all things in common.
May we give of our gifts and offerings,
    and distribute to all as each has need.
In Jesus' name, amen.

SENDING FORTH

Benediction (Psalm 23, John 10)

The Lord is our Shepherd.
We shall not want.
The Lord is our Shepherd.
In pastures green, we rest secure.
Our Shepherd leads us forth.
By still waters, we rest secure.
Follow the Shepherd,
in whom we find abundant life.

CONTEMPORARY OPTIONS

Contemporary Gathering Words

Do you need a guide?
The Lord is our Shepherd.
Do you need a doorway to new life?
The Lord is our Gate.
Do you need rest?
The Lord restores our souls.
Do you need care?
The Lord is our Shepherd.
Come; let us worship.

Praise Sentences (Psalm 23, John 10)

Jesus is our Shepherd.
Jesus is our Gate.
Jesus is the Way to God and safe pastures.
Jesus is our Shepherd.
Jesus is our Gate.

APRIL 20, 2008

Fifth Sunday of Easter
John A. Brewer

COLOR
White

SCRIPTURE READINGS
Acts 7:55-60; Psalm 31:1-5, 15-16; 1 Peter 2:2-10; John 14:1-14

THEME IDEAS
Hard as a rock. The psalmist considers God a rock fortress where protection may be found. Peter speaks of a cornerstone upon which the church is built—built of "living stones." The Gospel of John speaks of "my Father's house" where rooms are available and waiting for the arrival of the disciples. The stumbling block of 1 Peter may be tied to the gospel where Jesus says too plainly for some, "No one comes to the Father except through me." These weeks following Easter are a great time to remind our congregations that God is continually at work in our midst and is ever building the character of the church and of the individuals who are followers of the Way. Rock formations could be likened to the transforming work of God in the lives of those we serve. God continually is at work, changing us, calling us to maturity.

INVITATION AND GATHERING

Call to Worship (Psalm 31)

In you, Lord, I have taken refuge.
Let me never be put to shame.
Deliver me in your righteousness.
Turn your ear to me.
Come quickly to my rescue.
Be my rock of refuge,
a strong fortress to save me.
Since you are my rock and my fortress,
lead and guide me,
for the sake of your name.
Let your face shine upon your servant.
Save me in your unfailing love!

Opening Prayer (Psalm 31, 1 Peter 2)

O God of all creation,
become for us once again
the solid foundation upon which we build
our daily lives.
We gather before you,
this first day of the week,
to align our lives to the strong teaching
and life of Jesus Christ, our Cornerstone.
Receive our praise and thanksgiving
as expressions of faith and love.
We come to you, O Lord,
as people who desire to learn
and serve like Christ.
We are ready to receive your blessing
and direction today. Amen.

PROCLAMATION AND RESPONSE

Unison Prayer

O Lord, our Lord,
how majestic is your name in all the earth.

We pray this day
    that we may come to a clearer understanding
        that you have more interest in our character
        than in our comfort.
Where we have need of correction,
    speak plainly to us and grant us the courage
        to make the changes
        you would bring in our lives.
May the love we express for you
    on this Sunday morning
        continue throughout the coming week.
Strengthen this congregation, we pray,
    in order that we may become more effective
        in our ministry,
        in our service,
        and in our witness
            to the community.
In the name of the risen Christ, amen.

Passing the Peace of Christ

May the peace of the Lord be with you.
    And also with your spirit.

Invitation to the Word

Let the one who has ears to hear, listen.
The Word of the Lord speaks to
    the living of our lives today.
God's Word is our fortress and strength,
    providing shelter and foundation for daily living.
Let the one who has ears to hear, listen.

Response to the Word/Sermon

This is the word of the Lord.
    Thanks be to God.
This is the gospel.
    Praise to you, Christ Jesus.

THANKSGIVING AND COMMUNION

Communion Prayer (1 Peter 2)

O Lord,
    may we who eat this bread,
        become a people of living stones;
    may we who drink this wine
        become a people of salvation.
Enrich our faith and trust
    as we gather together again at your table
        for this sacred remembrance.
We confess our broken and sinful behavior
    and seek forgiveness for the harm we have done
        to others and to ourselves.
In these moments of communion together,
    may we experience the confidence of children
        who know they are loved and accepted completely.
Amen.

Unison Prayers of the People

O Lord, our Rock,
    we stand upon you alone,
        and upon no other.
Build our faith into a house
    made of living stones.
We offer these prayers of compassion
    for our families and friends.
Teach us anew
    that the foundation of life
        is love for you and for neighbor.
We pray for the community
    in which we live and work and learn.
Offer us, O God,
    at least one clear opportunity
        to be of service to someone in need.
Hear our prayers for those who are ill
    and who struggle to recover health and wholeness.
Let there be peace on earth,

and let it begin with us, today.
In Christ the solid rock we pray. Amen.

Invitation to the Offering (1 Peter 2)

We are better together.
When we join in music or mission,
or ministry or fellowship,
we discover that God makes us better,
being built upon one another
like living stones in the house of the Lord.
Let us join together now
as we receive the tithes and offerings
you have brought.
We have this common faith and common calling
to be in ministry—together.

Offering Prayer

Receive these gifts this morning, O God,
author of every good gift.
Out of the bounty of our hearts,
we respond with faithful generosity and love.
May these gifts become blessings for others
as they have been blessing for us. Amen.

SENDING FORTH

Benediction

Go now in peace.
Go now in peace.
May the love of God surround you,
everywhere, everywhere you may go.
Amen.

(Or)

May the love of God take away your millstones
and place you high up on the Rock,
that you may see more clearly

the calling of God in your life.
Into the hands of God,
  commit your spirit,
  in the name of Jesus Christ,
    our risen Lord. Amen.

CONTEMPORARY OPTIONS

Contemporary Gathering Words (John 14)

Come now and see for yourselves.
God is alive in our midst
  and begins life anew even among us.
You will see the very nature of God
  in those gathered around you.
Get ready to stand firm,
  to stand on the Rock that is Jesus Christ.
From there we will feel the confidence
  of those who follow the Way, the Truth, and the Life.
Welcome.

Praise Sentences

I will sing of God's love forever and ever!
Glorious things of you are spoken, O God,
  for you are trustworthy and true.
We praise you, O Lord, for your steadfastness.
You are faithful, and in you, we can surely place our faith.
I will sing of God's love forever and ever!

APRIL 27, 2008

Sixth Sunday of Easter
Mary J. Scifres

COLOR
White

SCRIPTURE READINGS
Acts 17:22-31; Psalm 66:8-20; 1 Peter 3:13-22; John 14: 15-21

THEME IDEAS
Living love is an ongoing theme in John 14 and in the Letters of John that appear later in the New Testament. Today's gospel reading integrates that theme with the presence of God's Spirit in our lives. Living love becomes a more realistic possibility when we realize that the Advocate is amongst us and within us. Living love emerges as the most fitting memorial we can offer to Christ, as we remember his death and celebrate his resurrection during this Easter season.

INVITATION AND GATHERING

Centering Words or Contemporary Gathering Words (Acts 17, John 14)
Search here for God.
Grope for truth.
But rest assured

that even as we search, grope, grasp,
wander and wonder,
God is with us, within us, and for us.
God is not far away.
No, God is as close to us
as our very breath.
For in Christ, who is God with us,
we live and move and have our being.
Because Christ lives,
we also live.
Because God loves,
we also love.

Call to Worship (Psalm 66, John 14)

Blessed be God, who calls us to love.
Blessed be Christ, who shows us the way.
Praise be to God's Spirit, who lives in our lives.
Praise be to God, who invites us to worship.

Opening Prayer

Spirit of truth,
speak to us in this hour.
Let your words
soak into our lives.
Let your Spirit
flow through our very being.
Let your love envelop us
that we may live your love
in all that we do
and in all that we say.
Amen and amen.

(Or)

Opening Prayer

God of heaven and earth,
gather us as one body.
Surround us with your love.
Strengthen us with your grace.

Open our hearts and minds
   to hear your words
   and to live your love.

PROCLAMATION AND RESPONSE

Prayer of Response
   Spirit of truth,
     we know that you have spoken
     and are speaking even now.
   Help us live these words we have so often heard:
     to love,
     to keep your commandments,
     to live in your Spirit.
   Guide our steps,
     that we may be your children,
     your people,
     your disciples.
   Help us live what we believe,
     that others may know your love. Amen.

THANKSGIVING AND COMMUNION

Invitation to the Offering
   As lovers of God,
     we are doers of the word.
   We keep God's commandments
     through our love for others.
   Let us take time now
     to express our love for God's world:
     in our gifts, our tithes, our offerings,
     and in our very lives
      given in love.

Offering Prayer
   Blessed God,
     let your love flow through these gifts we now give.
   As your children, strengthened by your Spirit,
     we offer our love and our lives.

Let our love be an instrument of peace,
    an expression of hope,
    a sign of your presence in the world.
In Christ, we pray. Amen.

SENDING FORTH

Benediction (John 14)
    Live your life in love.
    Love the life God gives.
    For in love, God is known.

CONTEMPORARY OPTIONS

Contemporary Gathering Words (Acts 17, John 14)
    The God who made this world
    calls us to gather this day.
        Gather us in, God of love!
    The God who made everything that is
    calls us to be a part of this creation.
        Gather us in, God of love!
    The God who is Lord of heaven and earth
    walks with us even now.
        Gather us in, God of love!
    The God who is Love Incarnate
    calls us to walk in love.
        Gather us in, God of love!

Praise Sentences (Psalm 66, John 14)
    Blessed be the God of love!
    Blessed be the God who loves!
    Blessed be the God of love!

    (Or)

Praise Sentences (Acts 17)
    The God of wonders is Lord of heaven and earth!
    Lord of heaven and earth!
    Lord of heaven and earth!

MAY 4, 2008

Ascension Sunday
Festival of the Christian Home

Sara Dunning Lambert

COLOR
White

SCRIPTURE READINGS
Acts 1:1-11; Psalm 47; Ephesians 1:15-23; Luke 24:44-53

THEME IDEAS
The psalm speaks of God who "chose our heritage for us" (Psalm 47:4). God claims us as God's own and we shout for joy. The Ephesians passage reminds us of the riches of God's "glorious inheritance among the saints" (Ephesians 1:18). Paul prays that we will be given the spirit of wisdom and revelation to know God through Christ and those around us. "Heritage" and "inheritance" remind us of the importance of family in our homes, and in our faith communities: mothers, fathers, sisters, and brothers. Christ our brother, and God our parent, are the ultimate examples of the connections we have with each other and of their importance in faith, hope, and love.

INVITATION AND GATHERING

Call to Worship (Psalm 47, Ephesians 1)

You have called us by name
and made us your children.
Shout to God with loud songs of joy!
You have chosen our heritage
and blessed us with your grace.
Shout to God with loud songs of joy!
You have given us the spirit of wisdom and revelation
to know you.
Shout to God with loud songs of joy!
We sing praises to God, the Mother of our love,
the Father of our faith.
Shout to God with loud songs of joy!

Opening Prayer (Psalm 47, Ephesians 1)

Holy One,
we come to worship today
expecting miracles
of life, faith, and hope.
We rejoice in the knowledge that you grant us,
and pray for the enlightenment
that will reveal to us
the power of your love.
As your purpose becomes clear to us
through the work of your saints in our midst,
may we know that we also are the image
of your love, hope, and faith.
We are your children now!

PROCLAMATION AND RESPONSE

Prayer of Confession (Ephesians 1)

Loving God,
once again we come to you troubled,
seeking your forgiveness.
In this place full of the promise of Christ's love,

we know you are here,
supporting us through the gifts
of those around us.
We feel a mother's love in the hug from a friend,
a brother's care in the offer of prayer.
Yet there are times during the week
when we feel empty.
Help us see, hear, and feel
the riches of our inheritance among your saints.
Help us nurture each other
to grow together in faith, hope, and love.
In Christ's name we pray. Amen.

Words of Assurance (Ephesians 1)
God's love is as unconditional as a mother's acceptance,
and steadfast as a mother's faith
in the goodness of her children.
Know that you are forgiven, nurtured,
and cherished always.

Response to the Word/Sermon (Ephesians 1)
Precious Lord,
let your words and our meditations
lead us in the way of your Son.
Remind us of our inheritance
as the saints of our day.
We are your body in faith and mind.
May we reach out to others
as examples of your hope and love in the world.

THANKSGIVING AND COMMUNION

Unison Prayer (Psalm 47, Ephesians 1)
Loving Parent,
we yearn to feel the warmth
of your peace in our hearts.
We pray for the spirit of wisdom and revelation
that will lead us to know you more deeply.

We give thanks for the examples of those around us—
> called by faith, led by Christ,
> and ruled by the Holy Spirit.
Steady us for the journey
> as we prepare to shout with joy!

Offering Prayer
> Accept these offerings, O God,
> > as gifts of our hearts.
> Bless them in their intent—
> > to honor you with our bodies, souls, minds, and faith.
> Put our gifts to work in our homes, our church,
> > and in the world. Amen.

SENDING FORTH

Closing Prayer (Psalm 47, Ephesians 1)
> God our Father,
> > lend us your grace
> > > to understand your word.
> God our Mother,
> > surround us with your love
> > > that we may surround others with ours.
> Strengthen us in knowledge, wisdom, hope, and faith
> > as we go out into the world.
> We praise your holy name
> > as ruler of all the earth. Amen.

CONTEMPORARY OPTIONS

Contemporary Gathering Words (Psalm 47, Ephesians 1)
> Rejoice in the knowledge that God loves you!
> > We are God's children now!
> Revealed in glory and love, God's purpose becomes clear.
> > We are God's children now!
> We are the image of God's love, hope, and faith.
> > We are God's children now!

Praise Sentences (Psalm 47, Ephesians 1)

Shout to God with loud songs of joy!
God is the King of all the earth and greatly to be exalted!
Christ is above every name that is named. Praise God!
Christ shows us the riches
  of God's glorious inheritance among the saints!

MAY 11, 2008

Pentecost Sunday
Joanne Carlson Brown

COLOR
Red

SCRIPTURE READINGS
Acts 2:1-21; Psalm 104:24-34, 35b; 1 Corinthians 12:3b-13; John 7:37-39

THEME IDEAS
Wind, fire, surprise, cacophony of languages, promises fulfilled, dreams, visions, gifts given and received, and most of all the Spirit—these are all parts of what make up the Pentecost experience, not only for the first-century church, but for us as well. We need to help folks experience these feelings with an intensity that may have been lost through familiarity. Let the rush of the mighty wind be felt, the flames seen, and the visions and dreams happen as we celebrate the gift of the Spirit in our midst.

INVITATION AND GATHERING

Call to Worship
Listen, can you hear the wind?
Come, Holy Spirit; come!
Look, can you see the dancing flames?
Come, Holy Spirit; come!

Can you hear the message
in a language you can understand?
Come, Holy Spirit; come!
Do you see the visions?
Can you dream the dreams?
Come, Holy Spirit; come!
Come let Pentecost become real in our lives this morning.
Come and worship our God who sends the Spirit
to touch us and transform us into Pentecost people.

Opening Prayer
Spirit of God,
we long to be open to your presence
in our church and in our lives.
Fill us with your wind and fire,
that we might be enlivened again.
Help us hear the words
as if for the first time,
that they might touch us anew.
Give us visions and dreams
of what you long for in your creation,
that we might begin to live them into reality.
Come, Spirit;
come into our worship,
into our church,
into our very selves. Amen.

PROCLAMATION AND RESPONSE

Prayer of Confession
O God, giver of the Spirit,
we sit surrounded by red
and hear the amazing story of Pentecost this morning.
But we've heard it so many times before.
It is so familiar;
we've ceased to be amazed and surprised
or filled with excitement.
Forgive us for our complacency.

Blow us out of our complacency.
Let the flames of passion dance in our lives.
Inspire us with visions and dreams.
Help us appreciate each gift you give us.
Help us be truly Pentecost People.

<u>Words of Assurance</u>
God has promised to send us the Spirit,
    that we might know fully
        God's presence in the world
        and in our lives.
Know that the Spirit of forgiveness and understanding
    flows over us this day and always.

<u>Passing the Peace of Christ</u>
Look around at all this wonderful red.
It symbolizes the passion of the Spirit in our lives
    and in the church.
Greet each other with that same passion and joy
    and celebrate that you are all here
        this joyous Spirit-filled morning.

<u>Invitation to the Word/Sermon</u>
O God,
    open our hearts and minds and souls
        to hear your word as if for the first time.
Help us experience anew
    the surprise and joy that your presence in the word
        can bring us.

<u>Response to the Word/Sermon</u>
Hear what the Spirit is saying to God's Pentecost people.
**Thanks be to God for this word of wonder
and delight.**

THANKSGIVING AND COMMUNION

<u>Prayers of the People</u>
For the gift of your Spirit in our lives and in our church…
we give you thanks.

For the gifts you give to each of us
to create your beloved community here on earth ...
    we give you thanks.
For all of creation, that it may be honored and preserved
and protected ...
    we give you thanks.
For the leaders of our nation and all nations of the world,
that they might be guided with wisdom and
understanding and committed to act in ways that bring
your presence and peace ...
    come, Holy Spirit; come.
For all places where there are wars and rumors of wars,
for those places where hunger gnaws,
for those places ruled by oppression and injustice,
for those places where hatred overcomes love ...
    come, Spirit; come.
Where dreams have died and visions are squelched
renew their spirits with your passionate fire ...
    come, Spirit; come.
For all who are ill, whether in body, mind, or spirit;
for all who mourn, whether for the loss of loved ones,
the loss of a job, or even the loss of faith,
fill them with your Spirit of compassion and strength
and healing, that they might know they are never alone.
    **Spirit, make us Pentecost people who reach out
    in love and caring.**
For all that you have given and will yet give,
we give you thanks.
    May we always be open to your Spirit. Amen.

Invitation to the Offering

Pentecost people!
We have received gifts too numerous to count.
Now we have a chance to give in thanks and joy.
Your offering will enable this church
    to be a Pentecost presence in this community
        and the world—

to reach out in passionate commitment
and bring the wind and fire of the Spirit
to a people and a world that so desperately need it.

Offering Prayer
For all you have given, for all we have received,
we give you thanks.
We bring before you our gifts of substance
and the gift of our lives.
We bring our passion and joy and surprise,
our visions and dreams.
May they refresh and enliven our church and community,
as the wind of your Spirit did long ago.

SENDING FORTH

Benediction
Go forth now as Pentecost people,
filled with the Spirit, dreaming dreams,
and seeing visions of God's possibilities.
**We go forth, knowing we are beloved and blessed
by a God who never leaves us alone.**
Go, to be surprised by the Spirit in all that you do
and everywhere that you go.
**We go, claiming our identity as Pentecost people—
people of wind and fire, dreams and visions,
people filled with that most amazing
and transforming Spirit. Amen.**

CONTEMPORARY OPTIONS

Contemporary Gathering Words
Wow! Rushing wind, dancing flames,
dreams and visions, everyone wearing red—
it must be Pentecost!
Come and expect the unexpected.
Come and be surprised by our awesome God
and that wonderful, transforming Spirit!

Praise Sentences

Give thanks for all of God's great gifts!
Praise God for the gift of the Spirit!
Come and be transformed by wind and fire,
by dreams and visions.

MAY 18, 2008

Trinity Sunday
Robert Blezard

COLOR
White

SCRIPTURE READINGS
Genesis 1:1–2:4a; Psalm 8; 2 Corinthians 13:11-13; Matthew 28:16-20

THEME IDEAS
Last Sunday, we observed the coming of the promised Holy Spirit at Pentecost. This week, Trinity Sunday now celebrates the fullness of the Triune God. Although the year A lections emphasize God the Creator, the second and third persons of the Trinity are specifically named in the New Testament readings and should be elevated in the liturgy. The emphasis on God the Creator may be best reflected in sermon, and in fact the long passage from Genesis offers rich preaching material.

INVITATION AND GATHERING

Call to Worship (2 Corinthians 13)
God the Creator is in this place.
The love of God is with us.
Jesus our Redeemer is in this place.
The grace of our Lord is with us.

The Holy Spirit is in this place.
The communion of the Spirit is with us.
We welcome the fullness of God's presence.
**God the Creator, Redeemer, and Sustainer
be with us now and forever. Amen.**

Opening Prayer or Closing Prayer (Matthew 28)
Jesus, our Savior,
in response to your call to be your faithful disciples,
we are baptized in the name of the Father,
the Son, and the Holy Spirit.
Open our lives
and teach us how to follow your great commission
to make disciples of all nations,
to baptize and teach them your ways.
Let us know the full blessings of our God—
Creator, Redeemer, and Sustainer.

PROCLAMATION AND RESPONSE

Unison Prayer (2 Corinthians 13, Matthew 28)
Hear, O friends, our God is one God,
and we are one people under God.
**We are called from all times and places,
from all circumstances and positions,
to be disciples of the Most High,
who is revealed to us in three persons.**
Hear, O friends, our God is one God,
and we are one people under God.

THANKSGIVING AND COMMUNION

Call to Prayer (Genesis 1, 2)
Brothers and sisters, let us lift up our prayers,
for our God hears them, every one.
The God who made earth and heaven,
sea and desert, meadow and mountain,
flower and redwood, snake and spider;

the God who blessed and placed every creature
in an interdependent web of creation,
this God listens to our prayers, every one.
Brothers and sisters, let us lift up our prayers.

Offering Prayer (2 Corinthians 13)

God, our Creator,
we call upon your name
and pray your fatherly protection,
your motherly nurture.
Jesus, our Redeemer,
we call you Lord
and submit our lives
as your disciples.
Holy Spirit, our Sustainer,
we need your guidance
to encourage and lead us on.

SENDING FORTH

Benediction (Matthew 28)

Let us go forth in the name of the Father,
the Son, and the Holy Spirit.
We will make disciples of all nations.
We will baptize and teach them of our God.
Remember that Jesus is with you to the end of the age.
Amen.

(Or)

Benediction (2 Corinthians 13)

The grace of the Lord Jesus Christ,
the love of God,
and the communion of the Holy Spirit,
be with all of you.

CONTEMPORARY OPTIONS

Contemporary Gathering Words (2 Corinthians 13)

Let's remember why we're here.

God has claimed us as family.

Baptized in the name of the Father, Son, and Holy Spirit,

we are daughters and sons of God forever.

So let's remember why we're here.

It's a family reunion.

Praise Sentences (Psalm 8)

How majestic is your name, O God, in all the earth.

All of creation tells of your marvelous works.

The heavens are the handiwork of your fingers.

All of creation tells of your marvelous works.

And yet you care for human beings as your children.

All of creation tells of your marvelous works.

How majestic is your name, O God, in all the earth.

MAY 25, 2008

Second Sunday after Pentecost
B. J. Beu

COLOR
Green

SCRIPTURE READINGS
Isaiah 49:8-16a; Psalm 131; 1 Corinthians 4:1-5; Matthew 6:24-34

THEME IDEAS
Even in the midst of our greatest despair, our worst national disaster, our most anxious personal grief, we need not worry, for God is faithful. After the long exile in Babylon, Isaiah proclaims that God will bring the Hebrew people home and restore their fortunes. In Psalm 131, David quiets his soul and resides in peace in the knowledge that Israel's hope rests with God. And in Matthew's Gospel, Jesus exhorts us not to worry, for God knows all our needs. If we love God, and forsake the allures of wealth and worldly things, God will provide all we need, just as God provides for the needs of the birds of the air.

INVITATION AND GATHERING

Call to Worship (Isaiah 49)
From the north and the south, the east and the west,
sing to the Lord.

Sing for joy, O heavens, and exult O earth.
Break forth, O mountains, into song!
For the Lord has comforted God's people
and has compassion on those who suffer.
Neither heat nor sun shall strike them.
Can a woman forget her nursing child,
or ignore the child in her womb?
Neither can God forget us.
Sing for joy, O heavens, and exult O earth.
Break forth, O mountains, into song!

Opening Prayer (Psalm 131)

God of mystery,
 calm our minds
  and quiet our souls.
Return us to that quiet center,
 where trust resides
  and worries fade away.
Like a weaned child with his mother,
 hold us to your bosom.
Like a weaned babe with her mother,
 wrap us tightly in your love and care.
Grant us your peace,
 that we might understand what is important
 and seek your kingdom. Amen.

PROCLAMATION AND RESPONSE

Prayer of Confession (Matthew 6)

O Great Provider,
 we love to worry:
  we worry about our looks,
  we worry about our health,
  we worry about our jobs,
  we worry about money,
  we worry about the future,
  we worry about worrying too much.
We act as if you do not know our needs.

We act as if the birds go hungry
and the flowers go unclothed.
We act as if you care more for the world around us
than you care for us.
Wake us up, O God.
Help us see our value in your eyes.
Help us feel your care for our every need,
through Jesus our Lord. Amen.

Words of Assurance (Isaiah 49)

The One who returns us from exile;
the One who sets the prisoners free;
the One who brings light
to those who dwell in darkness;
remembers us
as a mother remembers her children.
The One who offers forgiveness of sins
will pardon our weaknesses and bring us peace.

Response to the Word/Sermon (1 Corinthians 4)

Keeper of our souls,
you have made us stewards of your holy mysteries,
caretakers of your life-giving teachings.
May we treasure your charge,
and cherish your words,
that everything that is hidden from sight
may be brought into the light.

Call to Prayer (Matthew 6:25-26, 28-34)

Hear the words of Jesus:

Do not worry about your life, what you will eat
or what you will drink, or about your body, what
you will wear. Is not life more than food, and the
body more than clothing? Look at the birds of
the air; they neither sow nor reap nor gather into
barns, and yet your heavenly Father feeds them.
Are you not of more value than they? . . . And
why do you worry about clothing? Consider the
lilies of the field, how they grow; they neither toil

nor spin, yet I tell you, even Solomon in all his glory was not clothed like one of these. But if God so clothes the grass of the field, which is alive today and tomorrow is thrown into the oven, will he not much more clothe you—you of little faith? Therefore do not worry, saying, "What will we eat?" or "What will we drink?" or "What will we wear?" For...your heavenly Father knows that you need all these things. But strive first for the kingdom of God and his righteousness, and all these things will be given to you as well.

So do not worry about tomorrow, for tomorrow will bring worries of its own. Today's trouble is enough for today.

Free from worry, let us lift up our prayers,
and seek God's kingdom and righteousness.

THANKSGIVING AND COMMUNION

Call to the Offering (1 Corinthians 4, Matthew 6)
Holy One,
> teach us anew
>> that we cannot serve two masters,
>> that we cannot serve both you
>>> and our wealth and comforts.
We are stewards of your mysteries,
> custodians of your gifts.
Free us from fears of scarcity.
Free us from worry
> that we do not have enough
>> to give as we ought.
Touch our hearts with your generous Spirit,
> that our offerings may be a reflection
>> of our courage to serve one another,
>> as Christ has served us. Amen.

SENDING FORTH

Benediction (Matthew 6, Psalm 131)

Free from worry, we face the world unafraid.
Free from worry, we rest in the bosom of God.
Free to love, we go forth refreshed, body and soul.
Free to love, we face another week unafraid.
Go with God's blessing.

CONTEMPORARY OPTIONS

Contemporary Gathering Words (Isaiah 49)

Rejoice, you people of the north.
God's love is all around us.
Sing, you people of the south.
God's salvation is freely given.
Dance, you people of the east.
God's blessing rises like the sun.
Shout for joy, you people of the west,
God's love washes over us like the rising tide.
Rejoice, people of God.
Our God is an awesome God.

Praise Sentences (Isaiah 49, Matthew 6)

God loves us like a mother.
We love God like an infant child.
Worship the Lord, who greets us with loving arms.
Worship the Lord, who meets our every need.
Worship the Lord.

JUNE 1, 2008

Third Sunday after Pentecost
Mary J. Scifres

COLOR

Green

SCRIPTURE READINGS

Genesis 6:11-22; 7:24; 8:14-19; Psalm 46; Romans 1:16-17; 3:22b-28 (29-31); Matthew 7:21-29

THEME IDEAS

Even on this "ordinary" Sunday, when the scriptures each appear to be independent of one another, a common theme emerges. Our faith in God can be a rock, a refuge, a hope for the ages. God is faithful, and our faith in God's presence and God's teachings will sustain us through the many storms of life. Of course, sustenance may not always be luxurious. Simply surviving the great flood was no picnic: Noah and his family still had a filthy ship and a messy earth to deal with when the flood waters receded. Anyone who has visited a region in the aftermath of a flood or hurricane can attest to that reality. Still, survival in the face of great calamity and sustenance in times of poverty or want provide opportunities for better days, continued growth, and improved circumstances.

INVITATION AND GATHERING

Call to Worship (Matthew 7)

Built upon the rock of Christ's love,
our faith in God brings us to this moment.
We yearn for that solid foundation
amidst the shifting sands of life.
Come to Christ, who welcomes us
even when our faith wobbles.
We yearn for that welcome
in a world that storms with hatred and fear.
Christ our Rock holds us now,
even as God holds us throughout life's storms.
We come to be held, to worship, and praise.
We come with faith in God's love.

Opening Prayer (Matthew 7)

Rock of ages,
    hold us now.
Be the road beneath our feet.
Be the foundation of our faith.
Be the strength of our very lives.
As the sands of life shift all around us,
    help us remain steadfast and true.
As the winds swirl and blow,
    help us hear your Spirit's breath.
As we worship,
    help us rebuild our faith.
Shore up those places
    where doubt has crumbled our faith
        or shifted our priorities.
Center our focus on the foundation you offer,
    that we may live with Christlike love
        and rock-solid faith. Amen.

PROCLAMATION AND RESPONSE

Prayer of Confession

O God, our refuge,
cover us now.
Protect us from the glaring sun,
the blasting rain,
and the galelike winds.
Forgive us for the many times
we stray from your foundation,
and wander away from the cover of your love.
Forgive us when we build our lives
on beliefs that shift,
and on priorities that are like quicksand.
Offer your saving hand,
that we may walk away from treacherous places
and live in the safety of your love.
Help us trust the foundation of your ways,
and that love will survive
even the stormiest waters of life.
In the name of Christ,
the rock of our faith, we pray. Amen.

Words of Assurance (Matthew 7:24-25)

Hear Jesus' words of promise:
"Everyone then who hears these words of mine
and acts on them will be like a wise man
who built his house on rock.
The rain fell, the floods came, and the winds blew
and beat on that house, but it did not fall,
because it had been founded on rock."
With Christ as our foundation,
our sins are forgiven.
We will not fall.

Response to the Word (Matthew 7)

The wise build houses upon the rock.
Still, the rains of sorrow come a-tumbling down.

The wise build houses upon the rock.
Still, the winds of doubt storm all around.
The wise build houses upon the rock.
Still, the seas of life rage and roar.
The wise build houses upon the rock.
**May we be wise and not foolish,
building on the rock of God's love
and Christ's teachings.**
Though rains may fall, winds may storm,
and seas may rage, God's love will stand firm.

THANKSGIVING AND COMMUNION

Invitation to the Offering (Psalm 46, Matthew 7)
Proclaiming the gospel, rejoicing in Christ's glory,
and praising God's strong gift of refuge
and wisdom in our lives,
we bring forth gifts.
We offer our lives, built upon the rock of faith,
that God may use us and our gifts.
Through our giving,
may all see and know that the Lord of hosts
is with us now and forevermore.

Prayer of Thanksgiving (Psalm 46)
God, our refuge and our strength,
we behold your works
and are amazed at the many gifts
you bring in our lives.
We bring our gifts to you,
and pray that these gifts will truly glorify you
and exalt your name on this earth.
In Christ's name, we pray. Amen.

SENDING FORTH

Benediction (Matthew 7)
Let us be doers of the word and not hearers only.
Let us go forth as those who live Christ's love.

Let us be a people of rocklike faith.
We build a world that is founded on love.

(Or)

<u>Benediction (Matthew 7)</u>
The wise build houses upon rock.
The foolish build on sand.
With God's wisdom, we go to live lives of rocklike faith.
We go to build a world that is founded on love.

CONTEMPORARY OPTIONS

<u>Contemporary Gathering Words (Psalm 46, Matthew 7)</u>
Have you known a few storms this week?
Have you felt harsh winds blowing all around?
Here, a refuge of peace is ours.
Have you felt shifting sands as the years go by?
Have you feared the changes that swirl?
Here, a house of faith is ours.
Have you wandered the beaches of life?
Have you built on foundations that crumble?
Here, Christ our Cornerstone is our foundation
of rock-solid love.

<u>Praise Sentences (Psalm 46, Matthew 7)</u>
Praise Christ, the rock of ages!
Praise God, the foundation of life!
Praise the Spirit, a river flowing through us!
Praise God, whose love calls us here!

JUNE 8, 2008

Fourth Sunday after Pentecost
Mary Petrina Boyd

COLOR
Green

SCRIPTURE READINGS
Genesis 12:1-9, Psalm 33:1-12, Romans 4:13-25, Matthew 9:9-13, 18-26

THEME IDEAS
Central to these lessons is God's call to the faithful and God's promise for those who believe. Abram and Sarai answered God's call and by faith received God's blessing. Paul recalled their faith as he proclaimed the promise for those who trust in Jesus Christ. Matthew followed Jesus into a new community where God gathered society's outcasts. By faith the daughter of the synagogue leader and the woman with hemorrhages found healing and life.

INVITATION AND GATHERING

Call to Worship (Psalm 33)
Rejoice in the Lord, you righteous people!
Praise God with music and song!
God's word is faithful.
God loves justice and righteousness.

God spoke and created the heavens and the earth.
God's steadfast love fills all creation.
Happy are those who trust in God.

Opening Prayer (Genesis 12, Psalm 33, Matthew 9)
  Almighty God,
    we hear you calling us now.
  We come into your presence with joy.
  Guide us in this time,
    that we may know your plans for us.
  Give us the faith to do your work
    of righteousness and justice,
    that all creation might be blessed. Amen.

PROCLAMATION AND RESPONSE

Prayer of Confession (Genesis 12, Romans 4, Matthew 9)
  Loving God,
    you call us to follow you
    but we have so many excuses:
      we are too busy;
      our family needs us;
      we don't know the way;
      we're sure that we know what's best;
      we're afraid to leave what's familiar.
  Yet we need you:
    we need you to show us the way;
    we need you to heal our brokenness;
    we need you to give us courage.
  You have promised to bless us if we follow you.
  You have promised to be with us on our journey.
  You have promised to heal us.
  You have promised to bring life out of death.
  When we are filled with doubts,
    shine your light upon us.
  When we are in despair,
    show us how to hope against hope.
  When we treat others with disrespect,

teach us your mercy.
Forgive us; heal us; transform us,
     that we may be your obedient people. Amen.

Words of Assurance

Jesus Christ gives us abundant life, a merciful spirit,
     forgiveness for our sins, and healing for our pain.
We are blessed by God's love.

Invitation to the Word (Genesis 12, Matthew 9)

Open our ears, O God, to hear your call.
Open our lives, to feel your healing.
Open our hearts, that we may follow your word.
May these scriptures live within us
     as we journey together with you. Amen.

Response to the Word/Sermon (Genesis 12, Matthew 9)

Summoning God,
     as you called Abram and Sarai,
     as you called Matthew,
          you call to us still.
Healing God,
     as you healed the woman with the hemorrhage,
     as you gave life to a young girl,
          you heal our brokenness and give us new life.
Give us faithful spirits to follow you
     into places of newness and hope. Amen.

THANKSGIVING AND COMMUNION

Unison Prayer

God of blessing,
     you call us to venture into the unknown
          and trust that you know the way.
We are often afraid,
     reluctant to answer you,
     hesitant to take the risks.
Give us the faith to overcome our fears.

Remind us of your power to sustain us
    when we are weak.
Heal what is broken
    and bring us back to life.
May we live in the midst of your blessings,
    ever rejoicing in your love. Amen.

Prayer for Healing (Matthew 9)

Jesus, come to us now,
    we need you.
The woman with the flow of blood
    felt life seeping away
        until she touched you.
The ruler's daughter lay dead
    until you took her hand.
It is touch that heals.
It is your touch that makes us strong again.
Draw near,
    that we may reach for you.
Touch the tender places of our lives,
    that we might grow strong.
Heal our despair,
    that we may follow you with hope. Amen.

Responsive Prayer (Genesis 12, Psalm 33, Matthew 9)

We are your people, O God.
    You call us to follow you.
When we are afraid to answer your call,
    give us faith and courage.
When we feel life seeping from us,
    draw near that we may touch you.
When we feel dead and unable to respond,
    touch our lives with your love.
When we exclude others,
    correct us in your merciful love.
When we are lost in despair,
    teach us to hope against hope.

We are your faithful people.
We rejoice in your steadfast love.

Invitation to the Offering (Genesis 12, Psalm 33, Matthew 9)

Our God has healed our brokenness,
and has blessed us in so many ways.
Our God loves righteousness and justice.
In thankfulness for the blessings of healing and hope,
let us bring our gifts to God.

Offering Prayer (Genesis 12, Psalm 33)

God of our journeys,
you have blessed us
as we walk your paths of faithful living.
From the abundance of your gifts,
we present our offerings to you.
Use them for your work of justice and righteousness,
that all the world may know your steadfast love.
Amen.

SENDING FORTH

Benediction (Genesis 12)

God calls: "Go where I send you."
God will show us the way.
God calls: "Go where I send you."
God will bless us.
God calls: "Go where I send you."
God will bless all the earth.

CONTEMPORARY OPTIONS

Contemporary Gathering Words (Genesis 12)

God calls us into new adventures.
God calls us to leave what is familiar.
God calls us to follow in faith.
If we follow the call, we will find blessing.
If we follow the call, we will find challenge.

If we follow the call, we will find God.
Come; walk with God.

Praise Sentences (Psalm 33, Romans 4, Matthew 9)

Shout and sing for God is good!
Stand in awe of our amazing God!
Reach out to Jesus!
Feel his power!
Give glory to God!
God is able to do what is promised!

JUNE 15, 2008

Fifth Sunday after Pentecost
Father's Day

S. Kasey Crosby

COLOR
Green

SCRIPTURE READINGS
Genesis 18:1-15; Psalm 116:1-2, 12-19; Romans 5:1-8;
Matthew 9:35–10:8 (9-23)

THEME IDEAS
God's gifts to patient believers run throughout this
week's scriptures. God's unswerving and unconditional
love for God's people is shown in each reading. God's
love invokes a response of service in our hearts to the
many people around us. Since this is Father's Day,
the theme can include the gift of fatherhood and the
responsibilities that come with that blessing. This message is appropriate even for those who have never
been fathers.

INVITATION AND GATHERING

Call to Worship (Psalm 116)
Come gather before the Lord.
We call upon the Lord.
Come call on the name of the Lord.

We call upon the Lord.
Precious is the Lord to the faithful.
We call upon the Lord.
Come offer thanks to the Lord.
We thank the Lord.
Praise the Lord.

Opening Prayer (Romans 5, Matthew 10)
Justifying God,
    thank you for the peace you bring
      as we gather this day
      to worship you.
We offer praise for your gift of grace,
    even when we are reluctant
    to receive your help.
Help us rededicate ourselves
    to your calling:
      to help bring in your harvest,
      to witness to others through our words and deeds,
      and to courageously live our convictions.
Be present in our worship,
    and fill our hearts
      with the desire to serve you. Amen.

PROCLAMATION AND RESPONSE

Unison Prayer or Prayer of Confession (Matthew 10)
Creator God,
    when faced with your miraculous love,
      we often question our worthiness to receive it;
    when faced with opportunities to share your grace,
      we often retreat out of fear.
    when faced with your invitation to join the harvest,
      we often close our doors to the needy.
We focus our ministries inward
    to serve our own needs,
    rather than outward
      to meet the needs of others.

We ask for your forgiveness,
and for the strength to turn away from fear
and selfish motives.
Bless us so that we may open our hearts anew
and have the courage to serve you. Amen.

Words of Assurance

The Lord hears your voice in the wilderness
and grants the peace you seek.
Proclaim the good news!
In the name of our redeemer
you are forgiven.
Celebrate God's grace
and know that you dwell
in the heart of the Lord.

Response to the Word/Sermon (Matthew 10)

We hear your call to join the harvest.
Help us become your laborers in the field.
Help us greet the stranger, feed the hungry,
and clothe the poor.
With your presence and strength,
we will share your peace, your grace, and your blessing,
that all may know the glory of your love. Amen.

THANKSGIVING AND COMMUNION

Communion Liturgy (Romans 5)

Since we are justified by grace,
we share in God's love.
We are given peace with God
as we share God's love.
Come to the table and be renewed.
Come to the table and share.
Come to the table and feel God's love,
poured into our hearts through the Holy Spirit.
Come take the bread.
Come drink the wine.
Come to the table of grace.

Offering Prayer (Psalm 116)

What shall I return to the Lord
    for all of God's bounty?
The Lord hears my voice
    and listens to my prayers and supplications.
I will pay my vows in the presence of God's people.
I will pledge these tokens of my gratitude and love.
I will freely support God's harvest
    and ask that these offerings may multiply
        in God's ministry throughout the world.

SENDING FORTH

Benediction

Share with all the world
    the love you have received this day.
Take the blessing of the Creator,
    the grace of the Redeemer,
    and the love of the Sustainer
        as you leave this place. Amen.

CONTEMPORARY OPTIONS

Contemporary Gathering Words

Gather around the light that glows.
Feel the love that is here.
Gather around the spirit that flows.
Feel the love that is here.
Surround yourself with quiet peace.
Feel the love that is here.
Rest within God's embrace.
Feel the love that is here.
Open your hearts and minds.
Feel the love that is here.
Lift your voices in praise.
Feel the love that is here.
Gather around the spirit that flows.

Feel the love that is here.
(Alternative response)
Feel the love all around us.

Praise Sentences

Give thanks to the Lord for the gift of grace!
Praise the Lord for the call to serve!
Give thanks to the Lord for the gift of love!
Praise the Lord for the call of discipleship!

JUNE 22, 2008

Sixth Sunday after Pentecost
B. J. Beu

COLOR
Green

SCRIPTURE READINGS
Genesis 21:8-21; Psalm 86:1-10, 16-17; Romans 6:1b-11;
Matthew 10:24-39

THEME IDEAS
Happy readings these are not. In Genesis, jealous that
Hagar's son will one day inherit with her son Isaac,
Sarah asks Abraham to cast mother and son out into the
desert. Despite his distress, Abraham does so because
God says to listen to Sarah! As Ishmael lies dying of
thirst, God seems unmoved by Hagar's tears, and only
steps in to save mother and child upon hearing the boy's
cries. In Matthew, Jesus warns that he did not come to
bring peace, but a sword, and to set a son against his
father, and a daughter against her mother. Either God is
ethically challenged, or God's purposes are beyond our
simple delineations of right and wrong. In seeming
answer, the psalmist cries out in distress, pleading her
case before God, who is unlike the other gods—because
God hears our prayers and listens to the cries of our sup-
plications. God's ways are not our ways, but there is help
in the Lord and in no other.

INVITATION AND GATHERING

Call to Worship (Genesis 21, Psalm 86)

When we have been cast aside
in the desert places of our lives,
    you open our eyes to see wells of life-giving water
    to sustain us in our exile.
When our future seems lost
and others have taken our place of honor,
    you restore our hope
    and promise us an inheritance of our own.
Who is like you among the gods?
    Who answers prayer in our time of need?
We are here to worship you, O God,
    for you alone can save us.

Opening Prayer (Genesis 21, Matthew 10)

Eternal God,
    turn to us and be gracious to us,
    for we are beaten down
        and in need of your help.
Strengthen us for the journey,
    and show us a sign of your favor,
    that we may not be put to shame.
Comfort us, O God,
    and revive our souls,
    that we may have the endurance to take up our cross,
        and follow the one who leads us into life
            in your name. Amen.

PROCLAMATION AND RESPONSE

Prayer of Confession (Matthew 10:26)

Holy One,
    we hear your words and tremble:
        "Nothing is covered up that will not be uncovered,
        and nothing secret that will not be known."
We tremble, for there is much in our life

that we seek to keep hidden from others,
from you, and even from ourselves:
   our secret fears,
   our lurid fantasies,
   our smug satisfaction
     when enemies are brought up short.
Forgive our search for the easy way out:
   for easy answers,
   for the path of least resistance,
   for the surrender of treasured values
     to keep peace in the family.
Remind us that your Son came to bring us life,
   even if it meant turning son against father,
   and daughter against mother.
Remind us of our higher calling,
   and the promise of life in your realm
     which has no end. Amen.

Words of Assurance (Matthew 10, Romans 6)

Those who seek to preserve their life will lose it,
   but those who lose their life for Christ's sake
     will find it.
Those who have died with Christ through baptism
   are united with him in his resurrection.

Response to the Word/Sermon (Genesis 21)

It is hard to hear difficult news, O God,
   but we need reminding
     that your ways are not our ways,
     and that we rarely know
       what is good for us.
May hearing the story of Sarah's treachery
   make us freer to confess our own.
May seeing Abraham's refusal to stand up for his son
   inspire us to stand up for those whom we love.
And yet, may hearing these stories
   give us pause to wonder
     if our judgments and values

might hinder your purposes.
Help us discern your will, O God.
Help us know what is right,
    that we might follow the course
    that leads to life.

Call to Prayer (Psalm 86)

We lift up our souls, O Lord,
    for your goodness heals our ills,
    your forgiveness is sweeter than honey.
Your steadfast love
    strengthens all who call upon you.
Give ear, O Lord, to our prayers.
Listen to our cries of supplication,
    for you alone can hear us;
    you alone can mend our hurts;
    you alone can bind our wounds. Amen.

THANKSGIVING AND COMMUNION

Offering Prayer (Psalm 86)

Turn to me and be gracious, O God.
Give me your grace,
    and show me a sign of your favor.
Give me a sign,
    that those who hate me
        may see it and know that you help those
        who follow the ways of life.
Give me your grace, Lord,
    that I may offer all that I am
    and all that I have to honor you. Amen.

SENDING FORTH

Benediction (Genesis 21)

Though we have been cast aside,
you restore our future.
Though others seek to banish us from sight,

you bless us with opportunities for new life.
Go with the blessings of the One who loves us fiercely.
Amen.

CONTEMPORARY OPTIONS

Contemporary Gathering Words (Psalm 86)
I am poor and needy, O God.
I feel so alone.
You alone know my suffering, my pain.
You alone know the depth of my grief.
Raise me from the grave.
Raise me up from the death of superficiality.
You alone know my suffering, my pain.
You alone know the depth of my grief.

Praise Sentences (Psalm 86)
O God, you are great.
You do wondrous things.
Your strength knows no bounds.
You are our God.
O God, you are great.
You do wondrous things.

JUNE 29, 2008

Seventh Sunday after Pentecost
Mary J. Scifres

COLOR
Green

SCRIPTURE READINGS
Genesis 22:1-14; Psalm 13; Romans 6:12-23; Matthew 10:40-42

THEME IDEAS
Welcoming all, even the least and the littlest, prevails throughout Matthew's Gospel, but no more prominently than in these three verses. To welcome in Christ's name is an awesome task, and yet it is this task that calls us out of Christian community and into the world. To welcome in the name of discipleship is a joy-filled opportunity—both within our Christian families and outside of those familial bonds. For Jesus welcomed his sisters and brothers of the Jewish faith, right alongside the Greeks and the Gentiles, whom many called "pagan." To welcome all of these is a mighty challenge indeed. But surely such a welcome is nothing less than building God's realm here on earth.

INVITATION AND GATHERING

Call to Worship (Matthew 10)
Welcome, one and all!
Welcome young and old!

Welcome, great and mighty!
Welcome, humble and shy!
Welcome, big and bold!
Welcome, tiny and quiet!
Welcome, one and all!
Welcome to the household of God!

Opening Prayer (Matthew 10)
God of loving welcome,
 embrace us this day.
As you welcome us into this house of worship,
 so we welcome your presence into our lives.
Live in us; breathe in us; be in us.
Let your warm hospitality flow through us,
 that others may see your welcome in our eyes
  and sense your love in our presence.
Let welcoming love guide our worship,
 and may it be our way in the world. Amen.

Proclamation and Response

Prayer of Confession (Matthew 10)
God of loving welcome,
 we admit that we are not always as kind and accepting
  as Christ calls us to be.
We yearn to extend the hand of friendship,
 but sometimes shy away.
We cry for peace on earth,
 but sometimes wage war
  in our own cruel ways.
We seek community and love,
 but then offer only small parts of ourselves.
Where we are afraid,
 strengthen us to bravely reach out to others.
Where we are angry,
 love us that we may be kind and forgiving.
Where we are sad,
 comfort us that we may seek new joy.

Where we are in doubt,
  encourage us with your steadfast faithfulness.
Forgive us when we are not the welcoming disciples
  you yearn for here on earth.
Guide us to walk in your ways,
  that we may truly love and accept others,
  even as we have been loved and accepted by you.

Words of Assurance (Matthew 10)
  Whoever gives even a tiny cup
    of cold water to a small child
      is doing the work of God.
  We have received and given such cups
    many times over.
  Be at peace, for our sins are forgiven
    and we are restored to God through Christ Jesus,
    who is the living water that flows into eternity.

Response to the Word/Sermon (Romans 6, Matthew 10)
  Freed from the bonds of sin,
  we are welcomed as children of God.
  Freed from the fear of death,
  we are welcomed to live in joy.
  Offering the acceptance we have received,
  we share God's community of faith.
  Giving as we have received,
  we share Christ's community of love.

THANKSGIVING AND COMMUNION

Offering Prayer (Matthew 10)
  Welcoming God,
    there are many who need your welcome,
    who yearn for a taste of your love
      and a drink of your living water.
  Help us give of ourselves and our gifts
    with the same generous spirit you have shown us.
  In our giving,

may we welcome as we have been welcomed.
In our sharing,
may we love as we have been loved.
In these gifts,
may even the little ones know your loving welcome.

SENDING FORTH

Benediction (Matthew 10)
We have been welcomed and loved.
We go forth with welcoming love in our hearts.
Share this love with the world.
We will welcome even the least whom we meet!

CONTEMPORARY OPTIONS

Contemporary Gathering Words (Matthew 10)
Have you thirsted for a cup of kindness?
Have you hungered for a table that welcomes you?
Come on in …
for this is God's banquet of love and acceptance!
Welcome, one and all!

Praise Sentences
God is love, and we are God's people!
God is love, and we are God's people!
Loving one another, we worship the Lord!
Loving one another, we worship the Lord!

JULY 6, 2008

Eighth Sunday after Pentecost
Jamie D. Greening

COLOR
Green

SCRIPTURE READINGS
Genesis 24:34-38, 42-49, 58-67; Psalm 45:10-17; Romans 7:15-25a; Matthew 11:16-19, 25-30

THEME IDEAS
Emerging from each of these vivid texts is the power of discovery. The faithful servant stumbles across Providence's plan as he helps Isaac and Rebekah discover one another (Genesis 24). Yahweh's works exist to "make known to all people" the splendor of God's kingdom (Psalm 145:12). The Apostle discovers that regardless of intention, evil is never far away (Romans 7:21). Finally, Our Lord Jesus invites us to discover a secret— what has been hidden from the wise intelligentsia is given to those who would come to him (Matthew 11: 25b, 28).

INVITATION AND GATHERING
Call to Worship (Matthew 11)
"Come to me," Jesus invites.
We come to you.

"Come to me, if you are tired."
We come to you.
"Come to me, if you carry burdens."
We come to you.
"Come, and discover rest for your souls."

Opening Prayer (Genesis 24, Romans 7)
Like an oasis in the desert,
worship satisfies our sin-besieged souls.
Today, help us find the good in this life
by delighting in your presence,
and help us find the hope
you have placed in our innermost selves. Amen.

PROCLAMATION AND RESPONSE

Unison Prayer (Psalm 45)
In the adventure of life,
we have found you.
By your powerful grace,
you have found us.
As we proclaim your mighty deeds,
we celebrate your justice. Amen.

Passing the Peace of Christ (Romans 7, Matthew 11)
In the midst of sin, may you find peace.
Peace and forgiveness.
Fatigued by life's pain, may you find peace.
Peace and comfort.
Burdened by the law of do and do not,
may you find peace.
Peace and joy.
The peace of Christ Jesus be unto us all.

Invitation to the Word/Sermon (Genesis 24)
Almighty God,
prepare us to discover your word for us today.
Help us hear your servant,
and in the spoken words, hear your Word.

May these words help us recognize our master
in the many fields of life
through which we travel. Amen.

*Prayers of the People (Psalm 45, Romans 7,
Matthew 11)*
Thanks be to God, through Jesus Christ our Lord,
for the privilege of prayer.
Let us find our voice as we lift up our prayers:
Lift up your prayers for those who are burdened
by cancer, AIDS, Alzheimer's, and depression.
(Pause for silence.)
Lift up your prayers for those who are afflicted
with poverty, war, injustice, and the pain of loss.
(Pause for silence.)
Lift up your prayers for those who labor
to tell the gospel in all the world.
(Pause for silence.)
Lift up your prayers for those who carry the burden
of leadership in this church.
(Pause for silence.)
Lift up your prayers for the women, men,
and children in your lives.
(Pause for silence.)
Lift up your prayers for the deepest desires
of your hearts.
(Pause for silence.)
Thanks be to God, through Jesus Christ our Lord,
who hears our prayers. Amen.

THANKSGIVING AND COMMUNION

Offering Prayer (Genesis 24)
May the love of Isaac for Rebekah;
may the love of Rebekah for Isaac,
be present in our offerings this day—
offerings of our lives and possessions freely given.
May we be found faithful
with the many gifts you have given us. Amen.

Sending Forth

Benediction (Psalm 4, Matthew 11)
    As a gentle father,
        God has opened his hand
            and blessed us with his touch.
    As a loving mother,
        God has wiped away our tears
            and healed our every hurt.
    Let us leave this place now
        satisfied in his embrace.

Contemporary Options

Contemporary Gathering Words (Matthew 11)
    Open your mind, and let God teach you something new—
        about the holy one, and about you.
    Open your heart, and feel the thrill of God's words—
        whispering to you.
    Open your soul and experience spiritual rest—
        a gift to you.

Praise Sentences (Psalm 45, Romans 7, Matthew 11)
    Give thanks to God; alleluia!
    Through Jesus Christ our Lord; alleluia!
    For he has revealed himself to us; alleluia!

JULY 13, 2008

Ninth Sunday after Pentecost
B. J. Beu

COLOR
Green

SCRIPTURE READINGS
Genesis 25:19-34; Psalm 119:105-112; Romans 8:1-11; Matthew 13:1-9, 18-23

THEME IDEAS
God is the sower; we are the seed. Matthew's parable of the sower mirrors the reality of our world. The word of God simply does not seem to take root in some people; or if it does, it quickly burns out. And despite God's life-giving precepts and teachings, some people choose to follow their baser instincts, which Paul calls living according to the flesh (Romans 8). In the church, we believe that the soil of our lives can change. The cares of the world sometimes choke the word that people hear, but it need not be so forever. The church is called to be a place where people can find good soil so that everyone, regardless of past failings, has a chance to bear good fruit.

INVITATION AND GATHERING

Call to Worship (Matthew 13)
You are the Sower, O God; we are the seed.
In you, we live and have our being.

You are the Lover, O God; we are the beloved.
**In you, we grow into creatures more beautiful
than all the flowers of the garden.**
You are the Healer, O God; we are the healed.
In you, we find all that we need.
Come; let us worship our bountiful God.

Opening Prayer (Matthew 13)
Great Sower,
as seeds in your loving hand,
cast us upon the winds of your mercy
and help us find fertile ground.
May our lives avoid the stony pathways,
where the heat of the day's cares
strip us of our strength.
Keep us from the thorny gullies,
where life's snares choke the opportunity
for real growth in your Spirit.
Land us safely in rich soil,
that our faith may increase
and our joy may be complete. Amen.

PROCLAMATION AND RESPONSE

Prayer of Confession (Matthew 13, Romans 8, Psalm 119)
Holy One, Caretaker of our souls,
life in the Spirit hearkens,
but the allure of wealth and status
keep us mired in earthly passions;
righteousness and peace are within our grasp,
but the seduction of power and control
lead us onto paths of death and destruction.
Plant us in the rich soil of your church,
that we might blossom and bloom.
Do not give up on us,
for we are here to follow your precepts
and return to your ways.

Words of Assurance (Romans 8)

There is no condemnation
for those who are in Christ Jesus.
If the Spirit of God,
who raised Jesus from the dead,
dwells within us,
God will give life to our mortal bodies also
through the Spirit that dwells within us.

Introduction to the Word (Psalm 119)

Your word is a lamp to our feet, O God.
Your instructions are a light to our path.
Your decrees are our heritage,
our hope in times of trial.
Hold our hands and guide us,
that we might hear your words and live.

Call to Prayer (Psalm 119)

The wicked lay snares for us,
but in God we dwell secure.
The shadows of life threaten us,
but God is a lamp to our feet
and a light to our path.
Come; let us offer our prayers to God,
the One who brings joy to our hearts
and healing to our wounds.
Let us pray together.
*(The congregation may be invited to offer prayers of petition
and thanksgiving, followed by a period of silence.)*

THANKSGIVING AND COMMUNION

Call to the Offering (Matthew 13)

Like a field ready for harvest,
our lives bear the marks
of God's love and care.
We, who bear the fruit of God's labor,
rejoice as ones who have been blessed.

Remembering those who are in want,
we offer our gifts back to God
with love and thanksgiving.

SENDING FORTH

Benediction (Psalm 23, John 10)

Go, bearing fruit worthy of Christ Jesus,
a hundredfold, sixtyfold, and thirtyfold.
Our lives bear witness to the Sower.
Go, that your lives might be a beacon for all
who are snared by the cares and worries of this world.
Our lives bear the truth of the Sower.
Go, to bear witness that in God, new life is possible.
Our lives bear the fruit of the Sower.

CONTEMPORARY OPTIONS

Contemporary Gathering Words (Matthew 13)

We are like seeds on the wind.
The Sower has set us free.
We dwell among the rocky pathways
and the thorny ground.
How can we grow as we should?
In Christ, we find good soil.
God, sow us in this soil.
The Sower is here, that the harvest may be plentiful.
God, make us your harvest.
Come; let us worship the Sower, who gives us life.

Praise Sentences (Psalm 119)

God is our lamp.
God is our light.
God's word is life.
God is our lamp.
God is our light.

JULY 20, 2008

Tenth Sunday after Pentecost
Rebecca J. Kruger Gaudino

COLOR

Green

SCRIPTURE READINGS

Genesis 28:10-19a; Psalm 139:1-12, 23-24; Romans 8: 12-25; Matthew 13:24-30, 36-43

THEME IDEAS

Discerning the gates of heaven is a key theme emerging from today's readings. For a fearful Jacob on the run because of his deceit, suddenly there are God's angels, descended on a ladder to communicate awesome promises. For the Romans, fearful of suffering as Christians and living in a world of violence and anxiety, Paul points to suffering with Jesus as the very sign that they are truly Jesus' brothers and coheirs in God's kingdom. For the disciples, the wheat that grows and thrives, despite the weeds, is one assurance of the kingdom of heaven. Even in the midst of reversals—life's evil, its waste-lands, human sin and failings—even there we find the gates of heaven signifying God's consoling and powerful presence.

INVITATION AND GATHERING

Call to Worship (Genesis 28)

Surely God is in this place!
How awesome is this place!

This is none other than the house of God!
And this is the gate of heaven!
Let us worship!

Opening Prayer (Genesis 28, Romans 8)
God of our ancestors,
engrossed from ancient days
in the salvation of our world,
we seek you today
after another week of being on the run,
another week of trying to do the right things,
another week of trying to effect change.
We realize that what we do in hope
sometimes ends in futility.
We long for the fullness of your glory
and creation's redemption.
Open our eyes
to see your ladder stretching from earth to heaven,
to see the angels ascending and descending,
and to know that you are in our midst—
reliably, inevitably, bringing in your realm. Amen.

PROCLAMATION AND RESPONSE

Prayer of Confession (Psalm 139, Romans 8)
We are sometimes doubtful, O God,
that you are in our midst.
This weary, old world groans in pain.
And we humans are too often enslaved
by fear and suffering.
It's so easy to lose hope.
Search us, O God,
and know our hearts and thoughts.
If there is any wrong in us,
lead us in the way everlasting.
And teach us your hope
that shines even in seemingly hopeless situations.
Amen.

Assurance of Pardon (Psalm 139, Romans 8)

God searches us and knows us,
    and is acquainted with all our thoughts and ways.
The good news is that God forgives all our wrongs,
    and invites us to be brothers and sisters of Jesus Christ,
    joint heirs in all that is glorious.

Response to the Word/Sermon (Genesis 28, Romans 8, Matthew 13)

O God,
    we hope for what we do not see,
    but we have more hope for what we *do* see:
        gates of heaven in many places,
        sturdy wheat among the crowding weeds.
Open our eyes to discern your hidden presence among us,
    your shining grace and power at work
        in the most shadowed places,
    your blessing over even our stone pillows.
Open our eyes to see more fully, more truly. Amen.

THANKSGIVING AND COMMUNION

Invitation to the Offering (Romans 8)

Let us give generously,
    that others may experience our gifts
        as gates to heaven and find new hope.

Offering Prayer (Romans 8)

We give out of our longing
    for a world set free from destruction and decay.
With our gifts,
    open the eyes of those in need
        to your loving and powerful presence,
        and to your commitment
            to the glorious redemption
                of all creation.
With our gifts,
    awaken their hope and their strength. Amen.

SENDING FORTH

Benediction (Genesis 28, Romans 8, Matthew 13)
Wherever you may be,
may you see the gates of heaven.
Wherever you may be,
may you find the wheat among the weeds.
Wherever you may be,
may you turn stone pillows into pillars of God.
Go with eyes and hearts wide open
to God's lively presence!
Go in peace and hope!

CONTEMPORARY OPTIONS

Contemporary Gathering Words (Genesis 28)
Do you see the ladder rising in our midst,
rising to heaven, right in our midst?
Do you see the angels ascending, descending,
ascending and descending, right in our midst?
Do you see God standing in our midst?
Gates of heaven! Gates of heaven!
Right here! But not just here.
Do you see?

Praise Sentences (Romans 8, Matthew 13)
All who are led by the Spirit of God
are children of God.
We are children of God, heirs of God,
joint heirs with Christ.
Let us live in righteousness,
so that we may shine like the sun
in the kingdom of God!
May we be gates of heaven,
so that others may have hope.

JULY 27, 2008

Eleventh Sunday after Pentecost
B. J. Beu

COLOR
Green

SCRIPTURE READINGS
Genesis 29:15-28; Psalm 105:1-11, 45b; Romans 8:26-39; Matthew 13:31-33, 44-52

THEME IDEAS
"All things work together for good for those who love God, who are called according to his purpose" (Romans 8:28). These sentiments from Paul sum up the mood of today's scriptures. Laban tricks Jacob into marrying Leah rather than Rachel, but without this first marriage, we would not have ten of the twelve tribes of Israel. The psalmist extols God for the blessing of the covenant made with Abraham and his descendents. Paul expresses our conviction that nothing can separate us from the love of God in Christ Jesus. Finally, if we pursue the kingdom of God and treat it as a gift of great value we will have joy. Truly, all things do work together for good for those who love God!

INVITATION AND GATHERING

Call to Worship (Psalm 105)
O give thanks to the Lord; call on God's name.
Make known God's deeds among the people.

Sing to the Lord; sing praises to our God.
Tell of God's wonderful works.
Let the hearts of those who seek the Lord rejoice.
Remember God's strength,
the miracles God has wrought.
O give thanks to the Lord; call on God's name.
Make known God's deeds among the people.

Opening Prayer (Matthew 13)
Glorious God,
your kingdom is like a mustard seed
that grows into a great shrub
where the birds of the air can build their nests;
your kingdom is like a treasure hidden in a field
or a pearl of great value.
May we never be content
until we have forsaken all that binds us
and given all we have
to claim a place in your kingdom,
through Jesus Christ, our Lord. Amen.

PROCLAMATION AND RESPONSE

Prayer of Confession (Genesis 29, Romans 8)
Righteous God,
we are appalled at Laban's deceit,
giving Leah to Jacob in place of Rachel;
but we secretly admire his nerve.
We admire Jacob's willingness to work
fourteen years to marry the woman he loves;
but we secretly think anyone who willingly endures
a decade and a half of servitude is crazy.
Remind us again, that all things work together for good
for those who love you,
and who are called according to your purposes.
Help us discover your purposes for our lives,
no matter how foolish they seem
or how great the cost to ourselves. Amen.

Words of Assurance (Romans 8:29-30)

Who will separate us from the love of God?
**Neither death, nor life, nor angels, nor rulers,
nor things present, nor things to come.**
Who will separate us from the love of Christ?
**Neither height, nor depth,
nor anything else in all creation,
will be able to separate us from the love of God
in Christ Jesus, our Lord.**

Response to the Word/Sermon (Romans 8)

As God's chosen people,
hear these words from the Apostle Paul.
Those whom God has chosen
are predestined to be conformed
to the image of Christ.
And those predestined to be conformed
to the image of Christ are also called.
All those who are called are also justified.
And all those God justifies, God also glorifies.

Call to Prayer (Romans 8:26-27)

"The Spirit helps us in our weakness;
for we do not know how to pray as we ought,
but that very Spirit intercedes
with sighs too deep for words.
And God, who searches the heart,
knows what is the mind of the Spirit,
because the Spirit intercedes for the saints
according to the will of God."
Let us pray.
(A period of silence may precede the Lord's Prayer.)

THANKSGIVING AND COMMUNION

Call to the Offering (Romans 8, Matthew 13)

All things work together for good
for those who love God,

and are called according to God's purpose.
Let us approach God's kingdom
    as a treasure hidden in a field,
    joyfully selling all we have
        to buy that field.
Let us see God's kingdom
    as a pearl of great value,
    gratefully trading our worldly possessions
        for this one great prize.
Let us give back to God,
    as those who are offered God's very kingdom.

SENDING FORTH

Benediction (Matthew 13)
Like a treasure hidden in a field,
God has offered us the kingdom.
We will not shut out the lesson God teaches.
Like a pearl of great value,
God has offered us the kingdom.
We will forsake all lesser goods
to be part of God's kingdom.
Like a mustard seed that grows into a great shrub,
God has offered us the kingdom.
Amen.

CONTEMPORARY OPTIONS

Contemporary Gathering Words (Psalm 105)
Wake up and give thanks to the Lord.
We're not morning people.
Get excited and sing praises to our God.
Can't we just toast God with a cup of coffee?
Wake up and give thanks to the Lord.
Okay, okay, we're awake.
Praise the Lord!
Praise the Lord!

Praise Sentences (Psalm 105)

Praise the Lord!
Sing praises to God's name.
Praise the Lord!
Give thanks to God.
Praise the Lord!
Praise the Lord!
Praise the Lord!

AUGUST 3, 2008

Twelfth Sunday after Pentecost
M. Anne Burnette Hook

COLOR
Green

SCRIPTURE READINGS
Genesis 32:22-31; Psalm 17:1-7, 15; Romans 9:1-5; Matthew 14:13-21

THEME IDEAS
God's blessing and provision for us are common threads in these scriptures. God's blessing comes to those who cry aloud to God (Psalm 17:6); Jacob wrestles, and is rewarded with God's blessing for his perseverance (Genesis 32:29). The hungry will be fed, and the sick will be healed (Matthew 14:14, 19-20). God's blessing is so abundant that there is more than enough to go around.

INVITATION AND GATHERING

Call to Worship (Psalm 17)
Call upon the Lord, and God will answer.
**Show us your steadfast love, gracious God,
this day and always.**

Opening Prayer (Genesis 32, Psalm 17, Matthew 14)
Jacob was left alone, and a man wrestled with him until daybreak.

As you came to Jacob in the night, come to us,
that we may be satisfied when we awake.
Jacob said, "I will not let you go until you bless me."
The man said, "You shall no longer be called Jacob,
but Israel, for you have striven with God
and with humans, and have prevailed."
And there God blessed him.
As you blessed Jacob, bless us,
that we may behold your face.
Jesus saw a great crowd, had compassion for them,
and cured their sick.
As you healed the sick, heal us,
that we may tell of your wondrous love.
Jesus ordered the crowd to sit down on the grass.
Taking the five loaves and the two fish,
he looked up to heaven, blessed and broke the loaves,
and gave them to the crowd. All ate and were filled.
As you blessed the bread, bless us,
that we may be bread for the world.
Come to us, heal us, and bless us,
everlasting and merciful God. Amen.

PROCLAMATION AND RESPONSE

Prayers of the People (Genesis 32, Psalm 17, Matthew 14)

O God, hear our cries:
for those who hunger,
and those who are full;
for those who need you desperately,
and those who feel no need for you;
for those who wrestle with the impact
of being your blessed children;
for those who are unaware of your offered blessing;
and for concerns that are too difficult to express.
Hear our cries,
O God of our salvation. Amen.

Prayer of Confession (Genesis 32, Romans 9, Matthew 14)
Gracious God,
   provider of all we need,
      we are often content to rely on our own devices,
      our creativity, our cleverness.
We congratulate ourselves for our accomplishments,
   yet we find that these achievements and acquisitions
      do not fill the deep hunger inside of us.
We long for the Spirit bread you alone can provide.
Forgive us, merciful God.
Help us receive the blessings you offer,
   that we may be your bread for the world—
      blessed, broken for all.

Words of Assurance (Psalm 17, Matthew 14)
Hear the good news.
God's mercy is plentiful, and God's grace is abundant.
Receive the bread of forgiveness and steadfast love.

THANKSGIVING AND COMMUNION

Offering Prayer (Matthew 14)
Receive these gifts we offer, gracious God,
and multiply them to meet the needs in your world.
Amen.

Benediction
You have been fed with the bread of heaven,
and blessed by the presence and peace of God.
Now go into the world in the peace of Christ
to be bread for the world.
We go in Christ's name. Amen.

CONTEMPORARY OPTIONS

Contemporary Gathering Words (Genesis 32, Psalm 17, Matthew 14)
We come to this place with different needs:
some of us wrestling with problems

that threaten to overwhelm us;
some of us crying out for healing,
for relevance, for refuge;
some of us hungering
for what God alone can provide.
In this time and in this place,
God is here and meets us face to face.

Praise Sentences (Psalm 17, Romans 9)
Behold the face of God!
God's steadfast love is our refuge.
Behold the face of God!
God's righteousness guides our path.
Behold the face of God!
Bless God forever and ever.
(B. J. Beu)

AUGUST 10, 2008

Thirteenth Sunday after Pentecost
Erik J. Alsgaard

COLOR
Green

SCRIPTURE READINGS
Genesis 37:1-14, 12-28; Psalm 105:1-6, 16-22, 45b; Romans 10:5-15; Matthew 14:22-33

THEME IDEAS
Today's readings offer the familiar stories of Joseph and his amazing multicolored coat, and Peter walking on the water. Faithfulness in tough times is a common thread joining these two passages, as is the secondary theme of fear (Matthew 14:30). Joseph, betrayed by jealous brothers and sold into slavery, rose to become Pharaoh's right-hand man, saved all of Egypt from famine, and facilitated reunion with his family. Peter literally learns a lesson at the hands of Jesus when he begins to sink while walking on the water. How do disciples of Christ stay faithful to God and to each other when the going gets rough?

INVITATION AND GATHERING
Call to Worship (Psalm 105)
Give thanks to the Lord, for God is good!
We proclaim here and now

the marvelous works of our God!
Let our hearts leap for joy, O people of God.
We proclaim here and now
the marvelous faithfulness of our God!
God's ways are not our ways.
God's works are too wonderful to behold.
We proclaim here and now
the marvelous works of our God!

(Or)

Call to Worship (Romans 10)

The Word is near us in this place.
God's presence is everywhere.
We come to God's house to praise God's name!
The Word is near us in this place.
God's glory is everywhere.
We come to God's house to confess our belief
in the risen Lord!
The Word is near us in this place.
God's power is everywhere.
We come to God's house to believe in God!
The Word is near us in this place.
God's love and acceptance are everywhere.
We come to God's house to be saved!

Opening Prayer

Almighty and most gracious God,
we give you thanks for this day
and for calling us here
to your place of worship.
We gather to praise your name,
for your faithfulness endures
from generation to generation.
Signs of your faithfulness are all around us:
love, mercy, forgiveness, new life,
and the gifts of your Son, Jesus Christ,
and the Holy Spirit.

Help us claim your faithfulness
    as we seek to increase our faithfulness to you.
In Jesus' name we pray. Amen.

PROCLAMATION AND RESPONSE

Prayer of Confession (Genesis 37)
We have strayed, O God,
    from your will and your way.
Like the brothers of Joseph,
    we have betrayed family and friends
        for our own vainglory;
    we have enslaved others
        to suit our purposes;
    we have lied
        to cover our tracks;
    we have forgotten our faith
        when it is convenient;
    we have failed you and each other
        so many times.
Heal us, O God. Amen.

Assurance of Pardon (Genesis 37)
Here is proof that God's faithfulness never ends:
    that while we were yet sinners, God sent God's Son,
Jesus Christ, to shed his blood for our sins,
    that we might not be cast down into the pit,
    but rise with him to everlasting life.

Invitation to the Word (Matthew 14, Genesis 37)
God does not ask us for too many leaps of faith,
    but for small steps that help us stay with God every day.
Our scriptures today touch on familiar themes:
    fear, betrayal, lies, jealousy, and envy,
    but mostly, on the amazing faithfulness of God.

THANKSGIVING AND COMMUNION

Invitation to the Offering
There are many ways to respond to God's faithfulness,
    love, and mercy in our lives.

We come now, seeking to be faithful disciples of Jesus,
and to respond to God through our tithes,
gifts, and offerings.

SENDING FORTH

Benediction
May the God of Jacob, Joseph, Reuben, and Judah;
Peter, James, John, and Andrew;
Mary, Martha, Ruth, and Lydia,
grant you grace to abide in God's love,
give you peace to abide in God's forgiveness,
and the power to live in God's faithfulness. Amen.

CONTEMPORARY OPTIONS

Contemporary Gathering Words (Matthew 14)
Don't just sit there, do something.
But if we get out of the boat, we'll sink!
Keep your eyes on the Prize.
Okay, we'll place one toe in the water.
Tough times don't last, but tough people do?
For me and my house,
we will bask in God's faithfulness forever!

Praise Sentences (Matthew 14)
Jesus calls, "Come, get out of the boat.
Take that step of faith."
Thank you, Jesus, for the invitation!
Jesus calls, "Come, be my disciples."
Thank you, Jesus, for the invitation!
Jesus calls, "Even if you think you're not good enough:
come be my disciples."
Thank you, Jesus, for the invitation!
Jesus calls, "Come be my disciples."
Here I am, Lord. Praise your holy name!

AUGUST 17, 2008

Fourteenth Sunday after Pentecost
Laura Jaquith Bartlett

COLOR
Green

SCRIPTURE READINGS
Genesis 45:1-15; Psalm 133; Romans 11:1-2a, 29-32; Matthew 15:(10-20) 21-28

THEME IDEAS
It's just three verses long, but Psalm 133 still manages to communicate a joyful vision of God's kingdom. Paired with the Genesis story, we see a picture of a God whose love is so abundant that *all* sins are forgiven. We marvel at God's capacity for reconciliation, mercy, and unity, and we get a glimpse of the joy that's in store for us when we work together with God to fulfill that vision.

INVITATION AND GATHERING

Call to Worship (Psalm 133)
We have gathered from our different places
to worship here.
How good it is to worship together in unity!
We come from our different occupations,
our diverse activities.
How good it is to worship together in unity!

We come as unique individuals,
bound together in the love of Christ.
How good it is to worship together in unity!

Opening Prayer (Genesis 45, Psalm 133, Romans 11)
Merciful God,
    we boldly pray to you,
    confident that you will not reject us.
In spite of our human failings,
    your love continues to draw us together.
Be with us today,
    as we rejoice in the power of your love.
Sing with us today,
    as we proclaim the good news of your grace.
Dance with us today,
    as we celebrate the unity we share in Christ.
How good it is to be together!
Hallelujah! Amen!

PROCLAMATION AND RESPONSE

Prayer of Confession (Genesis 45, Psalm 133)
God of Love,
    we have come here today for a family reunion!
We know that we are sisters and brothers in Christ.
Each of us is your precious child.
And yet there is division in this family.
There is sibling rivalry, old resentments, new irritations.
We are quick to anger, slow to forgive.
We would rather choose our relatives,
    than acknowledge the all-inclusive nature
        of your family.
Open our hearts to your love,
    and show us the way of reconciliation.
Teach us to see each brother and sister with your eyes.
Help us claim our heritage as your own children,
    and live together in unity as your family.

Words of Assurance (Genesis 45, Psalm 133, Romans 11)

Do not be distressed or angry with yourselves,
for the God who reconciled Joseph and his brothers,
can surely reconcile us.
God's mercy extends to everyone.
Rejoice and live in unity!

Invitation to the Word (Genesis 45, Psalm 133)

Seeking unity, we come to the scriptures.
Open our hearts to hear and live your word.
Acknowledging our discord, we come to the scriptures.
Open our hearts to hear and live your word.
Realigning our lives with God, we come to the scriptures.
Open our hearts to hear and live your word.

THANKSGIVING AND COMMUNION

Call to Intercessory Prayer (Genesis 45, Psalm 133)

God of All,
gather us into a time of prayer
for our family.
Expand our vision
to understand each human being
as our sister or brother;
and enlarge our hearts
to offer love for each other,
even as you love each of us.
As we prepare to continue our family reunion
in our community and in the world,
be with us now as we pray for members of *your* family.
(Intercessions may be offered silently or aloud.)

Invitation to the Offering (Psalm 133)

Our hearts are overflowing with your love, O God:
like precious oil that cascades down
on the beards of old;
like the rains that shower down

upon your creation.
Guide us now, as we share with others
   the abundance of our joy.
We pray that you will give us the vision
   to use our blessings to offer hope to others.
In Christ's name we pray and act. Amen.

Sending Forth

Benediction (Genesis 45, Psalm 133)

It is time to take the party to the streets!
Go out to celebrate our common kinship
   as children of God.
Go out to tell the good news of Christ
   to every sister and brother.
Go out to let the power of the Holy Spirit
   unite us around the world.
Go out to continue this family reunion
   with all those who are longing to join the party.
Go out and rejoice!

Contemporary Options

Contemporary Gathering Words (Genesis 45, Psalm 133)

Mail out the invitations, blow up the balloons.
   It's time for a family reunion!
Cousins and grandparents, sisters and brothers—
hugs of joy for all.
   It's time for a family reunion!
Memories, stories, feasts, shared experiences.
   It's time for a family reunion!
Look around you and know
that we have come to celebrate.
   When the family of God gathers, it's party time!

August 17, 2008

Praise Sentences (Psalm 133)

How good it is when sisters and brothers
    live together in unity!
It is like precious oil, running down your head
    and dripping over your collar.
It is like the dew of Hermon,
    which falls on Zion.
From one side of the land to the other,
    we are bound together in Christ's love.

AUGUST 24, 2008

Fifteenth Sunday after Pentecost
Mary J. Scifres

COLOR
Green

SCRIPTURE READINGS
Exodus 1:8–2:10; Psalm 124; Romans 12:1-8; Matthew 16:13-20

THEME IDEAS
Each person has a role to play in bringing the realm of God to this earth. It took a village of women—the midwives Shiphrah and Puah, Moses's mother and sister, and the daughter of Pharaoh—to birth, protect, and raise Moses, the leader who would save the Hebrew people from slavery and oppression. It took Paul and the disciples to bring Jesus' proclamation of the kingdom of heaven to the thousands who would become the early church. It takes diverse members of the body of Christ—for this body called the church—to be all that God would have us be. Each person has a place in the realm of God, and each person has the ability needed to make a difference in this world.

INVITATION AND GATHERING

Call to Worship (Romans 12, Matthew 16)
We are called into this place,
a place to gather in community and love.

We are called into this body,
a body that is Christ's presence here on earth.
We are called into the kingdom of God,
a kingdom that is here and now.

Opening Prayer
Gracious God, our help and our hope,
be with us this day.
Bless our time together
as we seek your guidance
and grow in your grace.
Gather us as one body,
that we might be your kingdom on this earth.
In the name of Christ
who calls us here, we pray. Amen.

Proclamation and Response

Prayer of Confession (Exodus 1–2)
Merciful God,
hear our prayer.
When we have made lives bitter
with hard service or cruel words,
forgive us and guide us back
to your path of love and compassion.
When we have imposed ourselves or our agendas
on those around us,
forgive us and help us
to listen and cooperate with loving hearts.
When we have been the oppressor,
forgive us and redeem us
to be your people of justice and compassion.
In the name of Jesus, the Prince of Peace, we pray. Amen.

Words of Assurance (Psalm 124)
If it had not been the Lord who was on our side,
sin would have swallowed us up alive.
But thanks be to God who is on our side.

In Christ Jesus,
>the bonds of sin and death have been broken,
>and we are forgiven!

Response to the Word/Sermon (Exodus 1–2, Matthew 16)
>God of compassion and justice,
>>hear our prayer.
>As you first heard the cries of the Israelites in Egypt,
>>hear our cries for justice and compassion
>>>in your world today.
>Lift up those who suffer,
>>and guide us to be instruments of comfort
>>>in their lives.
>Bind us together,
>>that we might be the village who saves your children
>>>from despair and destruction.
>Guide us to be your kingdom on this earth,
>>that your will might be done,
>>and your kingdom might come,
>>>both now and forevermore. Amen.

THANKSGIVING AND COMMUNION

Offering Prayer (Romans 12)
>Christ Jesus,
>>we present ourselves as gifts to you.
>We seek to be your body on this earth,
>>and to live according to your good and perfect will.
>Guide us as your people.
>Help us use the gifts you have given to us,
>>that we might be instruments
>>>of your love and grace on this earth.
>In your holy name, we pray. Amen.

SENDING FORTH

Benediction (Exodus 1–2, Mark 16)

Blessed are you, children of God!
We seek to be God's blessing in the world!
Beloved are you, children of God!
We go forth with God's love and grace!

CONTEMPORARY OPTIONS

Contemporary Gathering Words (Exodus 1–2, Romans 12, Matthew 16)

Here in this place, God's light is shining.
Here in this place, Christ's voice is calling.
Now at this time, we are called to be God's justice.
Here in this place, Christ's voice is calling.
Within this community, we are Christ's body
here on earth.
Here in this place, Christ's voice is calling.

Praise Sentences (Psalm 124)

Our help is in the name of the Lord!
God will be our help!
Our help is in the name of the Lord!
God will be our help indeed!

(Or)

Praise Sentences (Psalm 124)

Blessed be the Lord of heaven and earth!
Blessed be the Lord of heaven and earth!

AUGUST 31, 2008

Sixteenth Sunday after Pentecost
Sara Dunning Lambert

COLOR
Green

SCRIPTURE READINGS
Exodus 3:1-15; Psalm 105:1-6, 23-26, 45c; Romans 12:9-21;
Matthew 16:21-28

THEME IDEAS
The underlying theme of these passages is that I AM WHO
I AM is with us always, leading us toward spiritual fulfillment and faith in action. Beginning with the symbol of
God's power and love in the burning bush, we are
reminded that we are on holy ground. The psalmist proclaims God's wonderful works: miracles and judgments
that make us stronger together. Paul gives us insight into
the true Christian spirit, which requires us to love one
another and overcome evil with good. Matthew illus-
trates the stumbling block that Peter became, and
encourages us to take up the cross and follow Jesus.

INVITATION AND GATHERING

*Call to Worship (Exodus 3, Psalm 105, Romans 12,
Matthew 16)*
Behold, we stand on holy ground.
O give thanks to the Lord.

178

Make known God's deeds among the peoples.
The strength and power of God's love
echoes through the ages to meet us here
in this place and time.
O give thanks to the Lord.
Make known God's deeds among the peoples.
I AM WHO I AM calls to us to remember
the Son sent to redeem us.
O give thanks to the Lord.
Make known God's deeds among the peoples.
We are ardent in spirit and in our love for one another.
We persevere in prayer and overcome evil with good.
O give thanks to the Lord.
Make known God's deeds among the peoples.
Let us enter into worship to rejoice in hope,
and take up the cross of Christ in our hearts. Amen!

Opening Prayer (Exodus 3, Romans 12, Matthew 16)
Blessed Redeemer,
    as we gather in this holy place today,
    may we feel your power surrounding us.
As we seek to fathom the message of the burning bush,
    calling us to greater faith and action,
    we are mindful of the struggle toward perfection
        expected of Christ's followers.
In the spirit of Moses, who heard the call;
    in the passion of Paul who fervently taught;
    and in the love of Jesus who gave his life,
    we come ready to listen to your word. Amen.

PROCLAMATION AND RESPONSE

Prayer of Confession (Psalm 105, Romans 12,
Matthew 16)
Holy God,
    we come to you
        remembering your wonderful miracles,
        and fearing your awesome judgment.

We are wholly dependent on your grace
and your nurturing faith.
We try, then fail; seek, then forget;
hope, then lose sight of your love for us.
Forgive our hesitation, skepticism, and despair.
Help us remove the stumbling blocks
placed in our path.
Strengthen us for the journey
toward faith, hope, and love,
that we may act for goodness in all we do.
We are your loving children. Amen.

Words of Assurance
In all things, at all times, and in all places,
you are forgiven.
The One who gave us life also sent us Christ,
that by his sacrifice on the cross
we are cleansed of all failings.
Claim this grace as your own
and go forward in joy. Amen.

Invitation to the Word (Exodus 3, Matthew 16)
May the Holy Spirit calm our hearts.
May God speak to our minds.
And may Christ center us in faith
as we search for deeper meaning
on our journey together.
Bless these words and open our eyes
to the lessons we are about to hear,
that we might recognize God's voice
in the burning bush,
calling us to action in the world.

THANKSGIVING AND COMMUNION

Unison Prayer (Exodus 3, Romans 12)
O Lord,
you promised a land of milk and honey

to the people of Israel,
you chose us as your people,
and led Moses with visual images
of your might and power.
Christ encouraged his disciples to feed the hungry,
love one another, and listen to God.
As we ponder these miracles,
we humbly beseech you
to consider these our prayers,
and to set us on our path toward righteousness.
We pray for our families.
(Pause for silence.)
We pray for our church.
(Pause for silence.)
We pray for our friends.
(Pause for silence.)
We pray for the world.
(Pause for silence.)
We pray for our faith and the journey to understanding.
(Pause for silence.)
O God, hear our prayer. Amen.

Offering Prayer (Psalm 105, Romans 12, Matthew 16)
Praise the Lord for these wonderful gifts,
given from the bounty of our lives!
Dedicate these gifts
to the service of Christ in the world.
With them we will hold fast to what is good—
extending hospitality to strangers,
and removing stumbling blocks for each other
in the world. Amen.

SENDING FORTH

Benediction (Exodus 3, Matthew 16)
Hear these words of exhortation:
to save your life you must lose it,
and in losing your life in Christ,

you will find life everlasting.
Recognize the stumbling blocks in your life,
  and recall the example of Moses,
  who recognized the voice of God
    calling from the burning bush.
By these examples, go with the assurance
  that I AM WHO I AM will be with you,
    now and forever.

CONTEMPORARY OPTIONS

Contemporary Gathering Words (Psalm 105, Exodus 3, Matthew 16)

We come to worship the God of the mountain,
  singing and making melody to the One
  who restores our souls.
We come to celebrate Jesus, the risen Christ,
  seeking to understand the will of the Savior
    that enlivens our minds.
We come to be filled with the Spirit of the burning bush,
  seeing in our pasts that power and hope
    that burns in our hearts like a living flame. Amen.

Praise Sentences (Psalm 105, Matthew 16)

Sing praises to the Lord,
  and tell of God's wonderful works!
Live in harmony with one another
  and let love be genuine after the example of Christ.
Followers of Christ,
  take up your cross and come!
Set your mind on divine things,
  and seek the presence of God continually.

SEPTEMBER 7, 2008

Seventeenth Sunday after Pentecost
B. J. Beu

COLOR
Green

SCRIPTURE READINGS
Exodus 12:1-14; Psalm 149; Romans 13:8-14; Matthew 18:15-20

THEME IDEAS
Love and judgment mark today's readings. God's love for the Hebrew people led to God's judgment against the Egyptians, who held them as slaves. The judgment that led to the death of the first born, the judgment that is celebrated as the Passover, is seen in Psalm 149 in the binding of unjust kings and nobles in fetters of iron. In Romans, Paul speaks about the commandment to love as a fulfillment of the law—laws against adultery, against murder, against stealing. Loving one's neighbor is itself a judgment against bad behavior. Finally, Jesus lays out how to deal with sin in the church. When one is judged to have sinned against us, Jesus' procedure ensures that future reconciliation will not be hindered by rumor and innuendo.

INVITATION AND GATHERING

Call to Worship (Psalm 149)
Praise the Lord! Sing to the Lord a new song.
Sing God's praises in the sanctuary.

Praise God's name with dancing.
Praise God with tambourine and lyre.
For God executes justice among the peoples.
Rulers feel the wrath of God's judgment.
This is the glory of God's faithful ones.
Praise the Lord!

Opening Prayer (Exodus 12, Psalm 149, Romans 13)
God of love and judgment,
> your love of the Hebrew people
> > led to your judgment
> > > against their Egyptian masters;
> your love of peace and justice
> > leads to your punishment
> > of nations and rulers
> > > who oppress the weak.
May we fulfill the law of law
> by loving our neighbor
> as we love ourselves.
May we put aside the works of darkness
> and put on the armor of light,
> that our love may be a beacon
> of your love.

PROCLAMATION AND RESPONSE

Prayer of Confession (Matthew 18)
Reconciling God,
> we would rather gossip
> > about those who sin against us,
> > than speak to them privately;
> we would rather parade our wounds
> > for all to see,
> > than quietly work toward forgiveness
> > and reconciliation.
Help us choose the harder road,
> the road that opens possibilities
> > for real healing, real forgiveness,
> > and real growth in your Spirit.

Help us place the best interests
of our community of faith
above our own need
for public vindication. Amen.

Words of Assurance (Romans 13)
Love does no wrong to a neighbor;
therefore, love is the fulfilling of the law.
When we live in God's love,
God's wrath passes over us,
as God's destroyer passed over the houses
of the ancient Hebrews.

Response to the Word/Sermon (Romans 13)
Take heed of the time.
Now is the moment to wake from sleep.
For salvation is nearer to us now
than when we first became believers.
The night is far gone;
the day is near.
Let us lay aside the works of darkness
and put on the armor of light.

Call to Prayer (Psalm 149, Matthew 18)
Be glad in your Maker;
rejoice in your King.
Make known your petitions to God,
· for whatever two or more of Christ's disciples
ask in God's name, it will be granted,
for Christ is among them.
Christ is among us now.

THANKSGIVING AND COMMUNION

Offering Prayer (Romans 8, Matthew 13)
As the ancient Hebrews offered sacrifices to you
in celebration of the Passover,
so we offer these gifts to you
in gratitude for your saving love.
As the Passover stands as a perpetual observance

for your love and mercy,
so may our offerings be a perpetual observance
of our gratitude for our calling in Christ.

SENDING FORTH

Benediction (Psalm 149)
God takes pleasure in us.
We go with God's blessing.
God adorns the humble with victory.
We go with God's blessing.
God takes pleasure in giving us the kingdom.
We go with God's blessing.

CONTEMPORARY OPTIONS

Contemporary Gathering Words (Romans 13, Psalm 149)
We are people of God's awesome love.
We're here to love others,
as we have been loved.
We are people of God's justice and mercy.
We're here to forgive others,
as we have been forgiven.
We are people of God's music.
We're here to sing and dance
to God's glory.
Praise the Lord!
Praise the Lord!

Praise Sentences (Psalm 149)
Praise the Lord!
Sing to the Lord a new song.
Praise God's name with dancing.
Make music to the Lord with tambourine and guitar.
Praise the Lord!
Praise the Lord!
Praise the Lord!

SEPTEMBER 14, 2008

Eighteenth Sunday after Pentecost
Mary J. Scifres

COLOR
Green

SCRIPTURE READINGS
Exodus 14:19-31, 15:1b-11, 20-21; Romans 14:1-12, Matthew 18:21-35

THEME IDEAS
Rescue and rejoicing are themes of the exodus from Egypt. Redemption and reclamation are God's gifts to the Hebrew people, just as they are Christ's gifts to the Christian people. God rescues the people from Pharaoh, and Miriam leads the rejoicing of her people. God redeems the Israelites from slavery and claims them as the people of God. Likewise, Christ redeems us and claims us as God's own children. The story of the Israelites' exodus from Egypt and Paul's proclamation of the gospel to the Romans both reflect these powerful messages of God.

INVITATION AND GATHERING

Call to Worship (Exodus 14–15, Romans 14)
Sing to our God of strength and might.
Sing to our God of grace and hope.

Sing songs of praise, glory, and joy.
Sing songs of grace, hope, and love.
Sing to our God, with songs of praise.
Sing to our God, with songs of grace.

Opening Prayer (Exodus 14–15, Romans 14)
God of redemption and rescue,
part the waters that overwhelm us.
Save us from floods of worry and confusion
that would keep us from following your paths.
Show us your powerful hand,
that we might live as people
of powerful hope. Amen.

PROCLAMATION AND RESPONSE

Prayer of Confession (Exodus 14–15, Romans 14)
God of power and might,
forgive us when we worship power for its own sake.
Forgive us when we forget the suffering
of the Egyptian people.
Forgive us when we live as if might makes right.
Forgive us; forgive us; forgive us.
God of grace and glory,
restore us to be people of amazing grace.
Help us remember that the good fortune of some
usually means less for others.
May justice and love guide our every step.
Restore us; redeem us.
Reclaim us,
that we might be people who walk on the dry land
of powerful hope and loving grace.
In the name of Jesus Christ,
forgive us and restore us to new life. Amen.

Words of Assurance (Exodus 14–15, Romans 14)
Sing praise to God, who has triumphed over death.
Grace has triumphed over sin!
In the name of Jesus Christ, we are forgiven!

Response to the Word (Exodus 14, Romans 14)

Loving God,
    help us welcome the weak
      and make paths for the wayward.
Help us live as people who not only follow you,
    but who lead others into your grace.
Let us live in you,
    always and everywhere.
Let your life and light shine through us,
    always and everywhere.

THANKSGIVING AND COMMUNION

Unison Prayer (Exodus 14)

Guide our steps, Shepherding God.
Direct us on your dry land
    into the promise of your salvation.
Let us live as people of the promise,
    that we may be generous friends,
      and faithful followers of Christ.

Invitation to the Offering (Exodus 14)

Bring forth your gifts,
    offer your lives,
    and God will transform them
      into miracles of hope!

Offering Prayer (Exodus 14, Romans 14)

Receive the gifts we now offer,
    that they may become the gift of hope
      to a world in despair.
Receive our lives as instruments of your grace,
    that we may become the gift of love
      to people who are hurting.
Receive us, redeem us, reclaim us,
    that we may be your people—
      a people of promise and hope.

SENDING FORTH

Benediction (Exodus 14, Romans 14)
Go forth into the wilderness of life,
    but wander not aimlessly.
Rather, walk with purpose and passion.
Live as people of powerful hope.
Give as people of gracious love.
Go forth with God!

CONTEMPORARY OPTIONS

Contemporary Gathering Words (Romans 14)
Welcome, all who are weak and strong,
    young and old.
For here, the weakest in faith
    are welcomed in the fullness of God's glory.
The youngest are included
    in all of Christ's grace.
And all are invited into life in the Spirit.

Praise Sentences (Exodus 15)
Sing praise to God!
Praise God's majesty and glory!
Sing praise to God!
Praise God's majesty and glory!

SEPTEMBER 21, 2008

Nineteenth Sunday after Pentecost
Hans Holznagel

COLOR
Green

SCRIPTURE READINGS
Exodus 16:2-15; Psalm 105:1-6, 37-45; Philippians 1:21-30;
Matthew 20:1-16

THEME IDEAS
Complaining to God is not always bad. In the wilderness,
it seems to have helped the hungry Hebrews. Before sending food, albeit with work required to gather it and with
conditions for its use (16:4-5), God proclaims, "I have
heard the complaining of the Israelites" (Exodus 16:12). In
fact, following God usually requires work—at its best, joyful, "fruitful labor" (Philippians 1:22). Complaining about
the good that comes to others in God's vineyard will not
get us far. "Are you envious because I am generous?" asks
the God character in Jesus' last-will-be-first parable
(Matthew 20:15). It is better to remember, with thanks, the
miracles of liberation, guidance, and nourishment
received by God's people (Psalm 105:1-6, 37-45).

INVITATION AND GATHERING

Call to Worship (Psalm 105)
Call on the name of God and give thanks.
Make known God's deeds among the people.

Sing and tell of God's wonderful works.
Let those who seek God rejoice in their hearts.
Let us worship God.

Opening Prayer (Psalm 105)
Liberating God,
we seek your journey.
With parted waters,
set us free.
With cloud and fire,
guide us.
With gushing waters,
quench our thirst.
With food from heaven,
feed us.
Draw us out with joy and singing,
that we might know your ways. Amen.

PROCLAMATION AND RESPONSE

Prayer of Confession (Philippians 1, Matthew 20)
God of fruitful labor,
work sometimes brings out the worst in us.
At home, at school, in the workplace,
even in our relationship with you,
we too easily question what others do and get,
instead of taking care of our own business.
Take away our bitterness.
Teach us the art of the careful complaint.
Give us grateful hearts, we pray. Amen.

Words of Assurance (Exodus 16, Philippians 1)
Hear the good news:
what we do matters,
but our salvation is God's doing.
God hears our complaints,
but also our prayers.
God will not forget us.
In Christ's name, we are forgiven. Amen.

Invitation to the Word (Exodus 16:1-15)
Like morning dew, like manna, fine as frost,
    may your word now cleanse and nourish us, O God.

Response to the Word/Sermon (Psalm 105)
Seek God. Seek God's strength.
Seek God's presence always.
Praise God! Amen.

Unison Prayer and Prayers of the People (Matthew 20:1-16)
God of grace and mercy,
    whether we are lifelong laborers,
    or new arrivals in your vineyard,
        we know you value us just as we are.
Hear now the prayers of thanks and concern
    that we now speak aloud
        or raise silently from our hearts.
(Petitions may be offered.)
God of the last, God of the first,
    God of all those in between,
    hear these concerns
        as we seek your presence in our lives
        and in a world in need. Amen.

THANKSGIVING AND COMMUNION

Invitation to the Offering (Philippians 1, Exodus 16, Matthew 20, Psalm 105)
Whatever our struggles, whatever our miracles,
    whatever our burdens, whatever our fruitful labor,
    we are thankful for the blessings from God
        and from God's good creation.
As signs of that gratitude,
    let us offer now our tithes and gifts.

Offering Prayer (Psalm 105)
God of abundance,
    receive these gifts
        with thanks from your people, we pray.

May they and we
   help your love and grace
      flow like rivers in deserts of need. Amen.

SENDING FORTH

Benediction (Philippians 1)
   Stand firm in the spirit;
      strive side by side;
      and live in a manner worthy
         of the gospel of Christ.
   Go in peace. Amen.

CONTEMPORARY OPTIONS

Contemporary Call to Worship (Matthew 20)
   Come at dawn!
   Come at noon!
   Come late in the day!
      Come to the vineyard,
      where the last and the first
      harvest God's good fruit together.
   Come!

Praise Sentences (Psalm 105)
   Sing and give thanks!
   Call on God, whose wonders guide us,
      whose rivers of love bless us.
   Sing and give thanks with joy!

SEPTEMBER 28, 2008

Twentieth Sunday after Pentecost
Shelley Cunningham

COLOR
Green

SCRIPTURE READINGS
Exodus 17:1-7; Psalm 78:1-4, 12-16; Philippians 2:1-13; Matthew 21:23-32

THEME IDEAS
What does being a servant look like? Philippians describes Jesus' servanthood as one of humility and obedience to God. In Matthew, John's servanthood comes from faithfully preparing the way. The servanthood of the two sons is judged, not by what they said they would do, but by what they did in the end.

INVITATION AND GATHERING

Call to Worship (Philippians 2)
Come, let us bow before the holy One.
Come, let us confess God's might.
Come, let us feel God's mercy.
Come, let us live in God's light.
As God's people, we lift our voices in praise.
Glory to you, gracious and loving God!

<u>*Opening Prayer (Matthew 21, Philippians 2)*</u>
Gracious Lord,
how shall we do your will today?
Will it be in acts of praise, in gifts shared,
in prayers lifted?
Who will you lead us to serve?
Help us trust you.
Help us listen.
Bless this community
as we come together in worship.
Encourage us, comfort us, unite us,
make our joy complete. Amen.

PROCLAMATION AND RESPONSE

<u>*Prayer of Confession (Philippians 2, Exodus 17, Matthew 21)*</u>
God of patience,
your people grow weary.
We complain and question.
We put you to the test.
Our mouths say yes,
but our deeds say no.
When we wander off your path,
when we fail to follow through on our good intentions,
when we give our attention to trivial things;
gently call us back to you.
Empty our hearts of anger and pride.
Empty our souls of greed and selfishness.
Empty our minds of envy, doubt, and mistrust.
As you poured out your very self
through your beloved Son,
pour your Spirit into our hearts today.
Forgive us our wrongdoing.
Reclaim us with your love.

<u>*Words of Assurance (Exodus 17)*</u>
Friends in Christ,
our God is patient, steadfast, and understanding.

Christ hears our cries of repentance.
The Lord knows our hearts, inside and out.
The One who created us promises to care for us,
    even when we turn away.
Hear these words of forgiveness.
Be strengthened to walk as disciples.
Trust in God's mercy. Amen.

Invitation to the Word (Psalm 78)

Speak to us, Lord, through these scriptures.
Remind us again of your everlasting power.
May we know your story and our place within it.
May we remember your mighty works and deeds,
    that we might know that you are the God of all ages.
May we claim your promise and share your love.
We are listening, Lord; speak to us today.

THANKSGIVING AND COMMUNION

Unison Prayer

Loving and merciful Lord,
    by your word we are nourished,
    by your hand we are fed.
Turn our hearts to you now,
    as we lift our prayers to you.

Offering Prayer (Exodus 17)

God of abundance,
    you fill us with good things;
    you satisfy our thirst;
    you meet our every need.
From your rock,
    our blessings flow.
Accept what we give in return:
    our hearts, our hands, our gifts, our love.
Use them to answer the cries
    of a world in need. Amen.

SENDING FORTH

Benediction (Philippians 2)

May you go forth with humble hearts,
ready to serve your neighbor and a world in need.
Amen. Lead us, O God!

CONTEMPORARY OPTIONS

Contemporary Gathering Words (Philippians 2)

Bend your knees!
Bow your heads!
The Lord, great and merciful, is coming!
The Lord, great and merciful, is here!
Open your hearts to God.
Open your arms to God's embrace.
For the Messiah calls you by name
and claims you as his own.
O Jesus, we exalt you.
O Jesus, we exalt you.

Praise Sentences (Philippians 2)

Praise Christ, who came as a servant.
Praise Christ, who was glorified by God.
Praise Christ, who reigns as Lord.
Praise Christ.
(B. J. Beu)

OCTOBER 5, 2008

Twenty-first Sunday after Pentecost
World Communion Sunday

Mary J. Scifres

COLOR

Green

SCRIPTURE READINGS

Exodus 20:1-4, 7-9, 12-20; Psalm 19; Philippians 3:4b-14;
Matthew 21:33-46

THEME IDEAS

As the ordinary season moves toward Advent, during a
season formerly known as "kingdomtide," the concur-
rent, independent scriptures become more overlapping
and interconnected. Such is the case today as the words
of Philippians reflect Paul's struggle to reconcile his his-
toric Jewish faith with his newfound faith in Christ.
Exodus offers us the center of Paul's former righteousness, the ten commandments. Psalm 19 celebrates the
perfection of God's law and praises the glory of God's
creation. In Matthew, Jesus forewarns that his own faith
community will reject him, even as he tries to live the
promises first given to the Hebrew people. And yet
the goal is steadfast through the ages: to press on toward
the goal of the heavenly call of God, reflected in the stories of Abraham, the commandments given to Moses, the

words of the prophets, and the promises of Christ Jesus. Living out the call of God, living in the way of God's kingdom, continues to be the pursuit of the people of God.

INVITATION AND GATHERING

Call to Worship (Psalm 19, Philippians 3)

The heavens are telling the glory of God!
Rejoice, for God's mercy is sure!
The earth proclaims God's amazing work!
Rejoice, for God's purposes are clear!
The day and the night reflect God's presence.
Rejoice, for God is among us now!
The sun and the moon shine with God's wisdom.
Rejoice, for God speaks to us now!

Opening Prayer (Psalm 19, Philippians 3)

Glorious, gracious God,
  shine upon us with your wisdom.
Call us into your kingdom.
Help us hear your words,
  that our hearts might be transformed
    into your likeness.
Help us know your grace,
  that our lives might be transformed
    into your love.
Speak to us now,
  that the clutter of our lives
    might be cleared away.
We want to know you.
We want to be like you.
We want to press on to the prize
  that is your kingdom on this earth.
Make it so, Lord.
Make it so.

October 5, 2008

Proclamation and Response

Prayer of Confession (Exodus 20, Philippians 3)
Okay God,
  we like to be right.
We like to have clear-cut answers.
Those ten commandments are pretty clear,
  yet even those challenge us each and every day.
Your law of love is clear more often than not,
  yet living love on a daily basis is tough work.
Forgive us for the times
  when we know precisely what we should do,
  and we do the complete opposite.
Forgive us when we knowingly wander,
  and guide us back when we are simply lost.
Help us always press on
  toward your path of love and grace,
  creating and molding our small bricks
    in the building that is your realm upon this earth.
Amen.

Words of Assurance (Psalm 19, Philippians 3)
Even as the words of our mouth
  and the meditations of our hearts
    seek to be pleasing to God,
    God is seeking to please us.
Through Christ Jesus,
  God has reached into our hearts
  and transformed our very lives.
In Christ Jesus, we are forgiven!

Prayer of Preparation (Psalm 19)
God of wisdom and truth,
  speak to our hearts,
    so that the words we speak,
    the words we hear,
    and the meditations of our very hearts
      might be pleasing and joyous to you.

THANKSGIVING AND COMMUNION

Call to Communion (Exodus 20, Psalm 19)

This is the table of grace.
In Holy Communion,
> manna in the wilderness becomes the bread of life
> > for all who call upon the name of Christ.

In Holy Communion,
> the law of the Lord becomes the law of love.

In Holy Communion,
> the promised land comes to us,
> that we might know God in the breaking of the bread
> > and the sharing of the cup.

Come to the table of grace.
Taste of the promise of God.
Feed on the law of love,
> and your cup will be filled with a living water
> > that never ends.

Communion Prayer (Philippians 3)

Gracious God,
> pour out your Spirit on these gifts of bread and wine,
> that they might become for us the bread of life,
> the living water that quenches our every thirst.

As we partake of these gifts,
> transform us that we might become your people,
> fed with the manna of Christ's grace
> > and the water of your everlasting love.

As we are fed and nourished,
> send us forth as people of grace—
> > people who answer the call to build
> > > your kingdom [realm] on this earth.

In Christ's holy name, we pray. Amen.

SENDING FORTH

Benediction (Philippians 3, Matthew 21)

Press on, dear friends, forgetting what lies behind.
We go forth, renewed and refreshed

to follow where Christ may lead.
Press on, dear friends, straining forward
with hope and courage.
**We go forth, carrying the promise of God
into the world.**
Press on, dear friends, building upon the promises
of Christ, our cornerstone.
**We go forth, living as people who wish to bring
God's heaven here on earth.**
Press on, dear friends, for you are the builders
of God's world!

CONTEMPORARY OPTIONS

Contemporary Gathering Words (Psalm 19, Matthew 21)

Are you burdened by rules and laws?
Come to Christ, the cornerstone of love.
Are you scared of your own need for perfection?
Come to Christ, the cornerstone of love.
Are you scattered and confused?
Come to Christ, the cornerstone of love.
Come to Christ, our Rock and our Redeemer.
For Christ's love is sure, and God's mercy is great.
There is no greater gift, and no greater reason for living.
Come to Christ, the cornerstone of love.

Praise Sentences (Psalm 19)

The heavens are calling ...
Praise God! Praise God! Praise God!
The heavens are calling ...
Praise God! Praise God! Praise God!

OCTOBER 12, 2008

Twenty-second Sunday after Pentecost
Hans Holznagel

COLOR
Green

SCRIPTURE READINGS
Exodus 32:1-14; Psalm 106:1-6, 19-23; Philippians 4:1-19; Matthew 22:1-14

THEME IDEAS
Today's encouragement to be humble and to focus on good things is especially apt in the heat of a political season. What if politicians, and all of us, would stand firm, but be gentle and thankful, thinking on what is true, honorable, just, pure, pleasing, commendable, excellent, and worthy of praise (Philippians 4:8)? What if seekers of justice and righteousness would first confess that "we and our ancestors have sinned" (Psalm 106:6), acknowledging the fallibility of people and nations as seen in the incident at Mount Sinai (Exodus 32:1-14)? Scholar Dennis Duling notes that even the harsh allegorical parables in Matthew 21 and 22, while illustrating the rejection of certain leaders, warn the newly included against self-righteous arrogance.

INVITATION AND GATHERING

Call to Worship (Psalm 106)
Praise the Lord.
Give thanks for God's goodness.
God's steadfast love endures forever.
Happy are those who observe justice,
who do righteousness at all times.
**Save us, O Lord,
and gather us from among the nations,
that we may give thanks to your holy name,
and glory in your praise.**
Come and worship God!

Opening Prayer (Philippians 4)
Gracious God,
  when the world's political noise is turned up high,
  we come not to escape, but to seek wisdom,
    and to focus on things that are worthy.
Dial down the distractions in our minds.
Tune our senses to your word
  and our hearts to your praise.
In your holy name we pray. Amen.

PROCLAMATION AND RESPONSE

Prayer of Confession (Exodus 32, Matthew 22, Philippians 4)
God of mercy,
  in our impatience for answers,
  we sometimes turn to idols of our own making
    and forget our covenant with you.
Passionate for what is right,
  we wrong those with whom we differ.
Pleased at the invitation to your banquet,
  we fail to arrive with humility and thanksgiving.
Forgive us when our faith is weak
  and our zeal too strong.
In Jesus' name we pray. Amen.

Words of Assurance (Philippians 4, Psalm 106)

Do not worry; the Lord is near.
God hears our prayers with compassion
and with abundant, steadfast love.
Rejoice, for in the name of Jesus Christ, we are forgiven!

Passing of the Peace (Philippians 4)

Let your gentleness be known to everyone,
and the God of peace will be with you.
The peace of Christ be with you.
And also with you.
Let us greet one another with a sign of God's peace.

Response to the Word/Sermon (Philippians 4)

Whatever is true, honorable, just, pure, pleasing,
commendable, and worthy of praise—
let us think about these things.
May we be strengthened to do what is pleasing
and acceptable in God's sight.

Unison Prayer (Philippians 4, Psalm 106)

In times of difference and division,
save us from rancor and meanness, O God.
Help us focus ourselves on things
that are excellent and worthy.
Make us witnesses to your way of justice
and righteousness.
Transform us and transform the world, we pray. Amen.

THANKSGIVING AND COMMUNION

Offering Prayer (Psalm 106, Philippians 4)

O God, creator of all that we have and all that we are,
no one can utter all your mighty deeds
or declare all your praise.
Yet accept these gifts, we pray,
both as tools of the work of the gospel
and as signs of our pledge to be coworkers
in Christ's name. Amen.

Sending Forth

Benediction (Philippians 4)
Do what you have learned and received
and seen and heard in Christ,
and the peace of God will be with you.
And may that peace,
which passes all understanding,
guard our hearts and our minds
in Christ Jesus. Amen.

Contemporary Options

Contemporary Call to Worship (Philippians 4)
Come, Holy Spirit, and incline our minds
to things that are true and just,
things that are pure and pleasing,
things that are excellent and worthy of praise.
Come, Holy Spirit, and incline our hearts
toward you!

Praise Sentences (Psalm 106)
Praise and thank the Lord, for God is good!
God is good, all the time!
All the time, God is good!
God's steadfast love endures forever.
Praise and thank the Lord!

OCTOBER 19, 2008

Twenty-third Sunday after Pentecost
Mary J. Scifres

COLOR
Green

SCRIPTURE READINGS
Exodus 33:12-23; Psalm 99; 1 Thessalonians 1:1-10; Matthew 22:15-22

THEME IDEAS
Jesus' clever response to the Pharisees reminds us that all of life belongs to God and that we are stewards of this life and its abundant gifts. Later in Matthew's Gospel, Jesus reminds Pilate that even the power of politicians is a gift from God. God's awesome power is recounted in Exodus and Psalm 99, and the power of God in our lives is referenced in the first letter to the Thessalonians. The power of God is yet another gift we are given as the Holy Spirit moves in our lives and in our world. This gift, like all other gifts we are given, is to be given to God and God's world as our way of glorifying God and serving Christ. Matthew's Gospel points to the wholeness of stewardship that Christ calls forth in our lives. The stewardship of all of life is no more and no less than what God asks for.

INVITATION AND GATHERING

Call to Worship (Exodus 33, Psalm 99, Matthew 22)
The earth has its kings, but God is ruler of all.
Praise God above all, the giver of life!
The mountains may tremble, the oceans may roar,
**but God's presence is more powerful
than the earth itself.**
Come into God's presence, for God is among us now.
O God, show us your glory; we seek your ways.
Come to the Rock, the God of life,
for God is present now.

Opening Prayer (Exodus 33, 1 Thessalonians 1, Matthew 22)
Loving, living God,
be among us now.
Show us your ways.
Guide our steps.
Live in us,
that we may be people of steadfast hope
and powerful giving.
Help us hear your words,
challenging us to give you
all the things that are yours.
Help us remember
that all we are and all we have
are gifts from you,
gifts to be shared in service and love.
Holy One among us,
help us be a holy people
who receive your word with joy
and live your message with love. Amen.

PROCLAMATION AND RESPONSE

Prayer of Confession (Exodus 33, Matthew 22)
Gracious God,
hear us now.

We want to know you.
We want to serve you.
We want to be like you.
But even as we yearn for this closeness,
    we are tempted to extol ourselves
        and pursue glory that is yours alone.
Help us when we close our minds.
Soften our hardened hearts,
    that we might regard everyone
        with the same love and grace
            that you show to all people.
Help us when we close our pocketbooks.
Loosen our clinched fists,
    that we might offer ourselves and our belongings
        as generously as you have offered yourself
            and your gifts to us.
Forgive us for past wrongs,
    and renew us to begin afresh,
        with steadfast hope and powerful love.

Words of Assurance (Psalm 99)
When we call to God, God answers!
God has heard our prayers.
In the name of Jesus Christ, we are forgiven!

Passing the Peace of Christ (Exodus 33)
In the face of a stranger,
    Christ is seen.
In the face of a friend,
    Christ is known.
Turn to those around you,
    and know Christ Jesus,
    as we share together
        the peace of Christ.

Response to the Word/Sermon (1 Thessalonians, Matthew 22)
God of grace and glory,
    help us truly hear the words

you have spoken.
Help us be people of constancy
in faith and in prayer.
Help us be people of dependability
in giving and in sharing.
Help us be people of steadfastness
in hope and in love.
Help us be the body of Christ,
your people on this earth,
bringing your realm closer to reality
each and every day.
Amen and amen.

THANKSGIVING AND COMMUNION

Invitation to the Offering/Stewardship (Matthew 22)
Christ does not give as the world gives.
Christ gives with abundant grace and unending mercy.
Even so, Christ asks us to give to God
that which is God's.
Is not all of life a gift from God?
Is not everything we own and everything we are
and everything we have somehow a gift from God?
Indeed, we are the stewards
of these amazing gifts from God:
pennies in our pockets, roofs over our heads,
paychecks that provide, talents that enhance.
These are God's gifts,
and we are God's people.
Just as we have received in great abundance
the gifts of love and grace of God,
let us give generously.

Offering Prayer (Matthew 22)
God of truth and justice,
help us be people of truth and justice.
Help us return to you
all that you have given to us,

so that your promise of truth and justice
    may come to fulfillment.
Accept and bless the gifts we now give,
    and bless us as we give even ourselves
      to your world.
In the name of the great Giver, we pray. Amen.

SENDING FORTH

Benediction (1 Thessalonians 1)

Go into the world, showering the world
with your works of faith.
    We go forth to serve as a labor of love.
Be steadfast in hope and full of conviction.
    **With joy, we depart, trusting God's guidance
    each day.**

CONTEMPORARY OPTIONS

Contemporary Gathering Words (Psalm 99, Matthew 22)

Christ is our Mighty King, lover of justice.
    Our God is an awesome God!
Christ is our God, holy and just.
    Our God is an awesome God!
Christ is our life, center of all creation.
    Our God is an awesome God!

Praise Sentences (Psalm 99)

The Lord is King!
Praise God's awesome greatness!
    The Lord is King!
    Praise God's awesome greatness!

OCTOBER 26, 2008

Twenty-fourth Sunday after Pentecost
Reformation Sunday

B. J. Beu

COLOR
Green

SCRIPTURE READINGS
Deuteronomy 34:1-12; Psalm 90:1-6, 13-17; 1 Thessalonians 2:1-8; Matthew 22:34-46

THEME IDEAS
God is faithful, but that does not mean life will be easy or even fair. We are called to love, but it is not always easy when things get difficult. In Deuteronomy, God takes Moses up a mountain to see the land promised to Abraham and his descendants—a land Moses will die within sight of, despite being the greatest prophet in Israel's history. The psalmist pleads with God to grant the people a year of blessing and peace for every year they have suffered evil. God is faithful, but a thousand years is like a watch of the night for God. God's time is not our time. Because of his love, Paul brings the gospel to the Thessalonians, despite his terrible treatment at Philippi. Good works are no guarantee of good fortune. Nor is love for others a guarantee they will treat us well; far from it. Despite seeking to teach us the ways of life,

Jesus suffers question after question from those who seek
to trip him up and discredit him. And still we are called
to love God and our neighbor as ourselves.

Invitation and Gathering

Call to Worship (Psalm 90)

Turn, O Lord! Have compassion on your servants!
Satisfy us in the morning with your steadfast love,
that we may rejoice and be glad all our days.
Make us glad as many days as you have afflicted us,
as many years as we have seen evil.
Let your favor be upon us—
O prosper the works of our hands!
Lord, you have been our dwelling place in all generations.
Have compassion on your servants!

Opening Prayer (Psalm 90)

Eternal God,
before the mountains were brought forth,
or ever you formed the earth and seas,
from everlasting to everlasting
you are God.
You turn us back to dust, and say,
"Turn back, you mortals."
For a thousand years in your sight
are like a watch in the night.
You make us like the grass
that flourishes in the morning
and fades in the evening.
Turn, O Lord,
and bless us with your favor.
Make our works prosper,
that all may know
that we are your people
and you are our God.

PROCLAMATION AND RESPONSE

Prayer of Confession (Matthew 22)

Eternal God,
  your patient love is like a mighty glacier,
  slowly pushing aside all that stands before it.
Be patient with us
  as we learn to love our neighbor
    as we love ourselves.
For we carry deep wounds and ugly scars
  from offering love
    to those who would hurt us.
Nurture us in your healing love,
  that we may be known as a people
    whose love for others knows no bounds,
    and whose fear holds no sway,
      through Jesus Christ, our Lord. Amen.

Words of Assurance (1 Thessalonians 2)

Just as we have been approved by God
  to be entrusted with the message of the gospel,
  we have been entrusted
    with God's commandment to love.
For in fulfilling the law of love,
  we fulfill all the requirements
    of the law and the prophets.

Response to the Word/Sermon (1 Thessalonians 2)

May our hearing of God's words not be in vain.
May we have the courage to declare the gospel
  to a world in need of good news,
    even in the face of great opposition.
May we be gentle in our instruction,
  like a nurse tenderly caring
    for her own children.
May our love lead us to share
  not just the good news of Christ's love
  but also our very selves in Christ's name.

Prayers of the People (Psalm 90)
Have compassion on your servants, O God.
Satisfy us with your steadfast love,
   that we may rejoice and be glad
   all our days.
Make your works known to us,
   and bless the works of our hands,
   that love may flow through us
   like springs of living water.
Let us enter into a moment of silence
   as we pray to the Lord,
   whose glorious power heals the nations.
(A time of silence may be followed by the Lord's Prayer.)

THANKSGIVING AND COMMUNION

Call to the Offering (Matthew 22:37-40)
Living according to scripture seems so hard.
There is so much contradictory advice,
   so many details,
   so many confusing injunctions.
Yet in a moment of breathtaking clarity,
   Jesus makes everything so simple:
      "You shall love the Lord your God with all your heart,
        and with all your soul, and with all your mind.
      And . . . you shall love your neighbor as yourself.
      On these two commandments
        hang all the law and the prophets."
In the spirit of the love to which we are called,
   let us give generously and lovingly
      to God and to our neighbor.

SENDING FORTH

Benediction (Matthew 22)
God's love has set us free.
God's love is upon us.

God's love has made us whole.
God's love moves within us.
God's love has called us to witness to a world in pain.
God's love sends us forth.
Go with God's blessings.

CONTEMPORARY OPTIONS

Contemporary Gathering Words (Matthew 22)
People of God, whom do you love?
We love the Lord, our God,
with all our heart, soul, and mind.
People of God, whom do you love?
We love our neighbors
even as we love ourselves.
People of God, whom do you love?
We love the One who calls us
and completes us in holy love.

Praise Sentences (Psalm 90)
God is our life.
God is our home.
God is our dwelling place.
God is our hope.
God is our life, forever and ever!

NOVEMBER 2, 2008

Twenty-fifth Sunday after Pentecost
Bryan Schneider-Thomas

COLOR
Green

SCRIPTURE READINGS
Joshua 3:7-17; Psalm 107:1-7, 33-37; 1 Thessalonians 2: 9-13; Matthew 23:1-12

THEME IDEAS
The gospel lesson may provide the setting to reflect upon the broad nature of the church or the community of God. Within this context, the other scriptures offer insight and commentary. Joshua 3:7-17 and Psalm 107 speak of God's abiding presence that guides this community. First Thessalonians 2:9-13 offers a glimpse at the nature of the community founded on God's word. Matthew 23:1-12 speaks of how we are to act and view ourselves.

INVITATION AND GATHERING

Call to Worship (Psalm 107)
Give thanks to God.
   God's steadfast love endures forever.
With holy hands we are protected.
   God turns desert wastes into beautiful gardens.
Give thanks to God.
   God's steadfast love endures forever.

Opening Prayer (Joshua 3)
> Almighty God,
>> your abiding presence guides your people
>>> through the wilderness and into the promised land.
>> May we witness your steadfast love with us today,
>>> guiding us to walk as your children,
>>> servants of Christ and of each other. Amen.

PROCLAMATION AND RESPONSE

Unison Prayer (1 Thessalonians 2)
> Holy God, you care for us as a loving parent,
>> that we might do the same for others.
> Help us so proclaim and bear witness to the gospel,
>> that all might recognize your word.
> Strengthen us to be pure, upright
>> and blameless before others,
> that nothing may hinder your teachings.
> **In our churches, may the word be taught.**
> **In our lives, may the word be seen.**
> **In our hearts, may the word dwell forever. Amen.**

Invitation to the Word
> *(The following lines may be used together prior to all of the
> readings or individually before each scripture reading.)*
> Hear the word of God,
>> that you might walk in holiness all your days.
> Receive the word of God,
>> that it might be at work within you.
> Heed the word of God,
>> that you may become its servant.

Response to the Word/Sermon (1 Thessalonians 2)
> By the word, God calls us into covenant.
> **May we receive the divine word**
>> **that it might be at work within us.**
> **May we be receptive students of it.**
> **May it show us the call of service**
>> **in Christ's holy church.**

219

THANKSGIVING AND COMMUNION

Invitation to the Offering
We are the church, called to serve.
Our service begins by offering our lives to Christ,
    and continues through the gifts we give,
    that the church may continue to witness
        to the word of God.

Offering Prayer
To you we offer our praise.
For you we offer gifts from our lives.
With you we live in service to the world.
Lord Jesus Christ,
    teach us to proclaim your word in a hurting world,
    not only in word, but in action and service,
    that all we do might be an offering to you.

SENDING FORTH

Benediction
May God's steadfast love keep you from all harm
    and lead you in Christ's service this week.

CONTEMPORARY OPTIONS

Contemporary Gathering Words
Through stories of faith and acts of grace,
we are reminded that God is always here.
By God's presence we are guided.
Through God's word we are instructed.
With God's Spirit we are formed.
Come, let us lift our voices in praise
and offer our lives in service to God.

Praise Sentences (Psalm 107, Matthew 23)
God's love is forever.
God's word is with us.
Hear God's word calling to us:
    "All who humble themselves will be exalted."

NOVEMBER 9, 2008

Twenty-sixth Sunday after Pentecost
Laura Jaquith Bartlett

COLOR
Green

SCRIPTURE READINGS
Joshua 24:1-3a, 14-25; Psalm 78:1-7; 1 Thessalonians 4: 13-18; Matthew 25:1-13

THEME IDEAS
We will tell about the Lord from generation to genera-tion, says the psalmist; but the truth is sometimes our passion for the story wears a bit thin. We start taking God for granted. Today's scriptures remind us that we need persistence, patience, and faithfulness for the long haul. Joshua's people promised long ago to witness to God; there was no stop date on that covenant. Reading the Matthew passage, we realize that we've been hearing this "Christ is coming" stuff for years—but do we live as if we still believe it? As Advent approaches, our worship can help us reclaim our passion.

INVITATION AND GATHERING
Call to Worship (Joshua 24, Psalm 78, 1 Thessalonians 4)
The God of our ancestors has led us to this place.
We are witnesses.

We have sworn to teach God's promises
to all generations.
We are witnesses.
The time is coming when Christ will come again in glory.
We are witnesses.
Let us tell the world of God's faithful love.
We will worship and witness together!

Opening Prayer (1 Thessalonians 4, Matthew 25)
Your love has brought us together, O Lord,
and it is your love that sustains us through each day.
We pray that you would keep us faithful.
Even as we watch for signs of your kingdom,
strengthen us to work with you
to bring about, here and now,
your reign on earth.
Give us the courage
to witness to your presence in the world,
today, tomorrow, and into the future.
We pray in the name of the One who comes,
Christ our Savior. Amen.

PROCLAMATION AND RESPONSE

Prayer of Confession (Joshua 24, Matthew 25)
God of Mystery,
we want to stay awake
and be ready for your surprises,
but we are tired and overcome
with the usual routine.
We want to wait patiently
for the fulfillment of your kingdom,
but we are frustrated by our need
for immediate gratification.
We want to believe your promises from ancient days,
but we are overwhelmed with postmodern doubts.
Come to us again, O God.
Awaken us with your unexpected grace.

Shock us with your daring mercy.
Lift us up from lethargy
    and set our feet on your path once more.
(Prayer continues in silence.)

Words of Assurance (1 Thessalonians 4)

Encourage one another with these words:
    "We will be with the Lord forever."
God's promises are never forgotten.
Do not grieve as those who have no hope.
Our hope is in God,
    and not even death can overcome that hope.
Enter into God's mercy and love!

Invitation to the Word

(A dialogue for two readers)
Hey, wake up! It's time for the sermon.
    What do you mean, wake up?
    This is prime nap time!
How can you sleep at a time like this?
You might miss something important!
    Nah, I've been hearing this same old stuff all my life.
But this is God's word!
Don't you know this could change your life?
    Change my life?!
    Uh ... I must have missed that part.
Exactly! We've promised to serve God,
to be witnesses with our lives.
How can you witness when you're asleep?
    Well, I guess it might not hurt to pay attention ....
    just this once.
Pay attention today and every day!
This is the word of God!
    And you never know what might happen.

THANKSGIVING AND COMMUNION

Prayers of the People (Matthew 25)

O Lord,
  we wait for you to come again into our midst.
Sometimes we wait patiently, sometimes not.
Always we are aware of how much the world needs you.
We pray today for those in our community
  who need your healing and comfort.
(Pause for silence.)
We pray for persons in leadership across our country,
  that together we might make wise decisions.
(Pause for silence.)
We pray for brothers and sisters around the world,
  whose lives are torn apart by war.
(Pause for silence.)
We pray for the saints who have witnessed to your love.
(Pause for silence.)
We pray, knowing that you are with us now,
  and that you will strengthen us to keep awake,
  to keep the faith,
  to keep working for the time
    when Christ will come again to surprise us anew
      with love and justice on earth. Amen.

Offering Prayer (Joshua 24)

We dedicate these gifts to you, Generous God,
  even as we dedicate our lives to you.
Keep us true to our promise,
  that we may witness to you
    with all that we are and all that we do. Amen.

SENDING FORTH

Benediction (Matthew 25)

Go out to stay awake! Go out to keep alert and be ready!
We do not know the day or the hour,

but we do know that God goes with us at all hours, on all days.
Go with the love of God, the peace of Christ,
and the communion of the Holy Spirit.
We go to witness and serve! Amen.

CONTEMPORARY OPTIONS

Contemporary Gathering Words (Matthew 25)
(Each line could be read by a different voice.)
It is time to wake up,
   for God is about to surprise us.
It is time to prepare,
   for God's love is about to change the world.
It is time to get ready,
   for God needs us to proclaim the good news.
It is time to start planning,
   for God's invitation will fill our church.
It is time to worship,
   for God is here now!

Praise Sentences (Joshua 24, 1 Thessalonians 4)
It is the Lord our God who brought us and our ancestors
   up from the land of Egypt,
   out of the house of slavery,
   and who did great signs in our midst.
It is the Lord our God who has protected us
   and loved us through all the years.
It is the Lord our God whose own Son, Jesus Christ,
   died and rose again, conquering death.
It is the Lord our God whom we worship today. Amen!

NOVEMBER 16, 2008

Twenty-seventh Sunday after Pentecost
Mary J. Scifres

COLOR
Green

SCRIPTURE READINGS
Judges 4:1-7; Psalm 123; 1 Thessalonians 5:1-11; Matthew 25:14-30

THEME IDEAS
Awareness is a crucial component of the Christian life. In Thessalonians, we are called to "be awake!" In the parable of the Talents, we are reminded to be aware of our God-given gifts and the responsibilities they bring. Christ calls us to recognize and utilize those gifts. The psalmist reminds us to lift our eyes and look for God's help. Even to be a successful leader and judge, the prophetess Deborah had to be constantly aware of God's guidance, if Israel was to escape oppression. To follow God's guidance, we must first be aware of God's presence. To respond to Christ's call, we must first listen and hear that call. To multiply our gifts, we must recognize our gifts and use them for God's glory.

INVITATION AND GATHERING

Call to Worship (Psalm 123, Matthew 25)

Open your eyes! Christ is in this room!
Open my eyes? But it's Sunday morning!
Open your ears! Christ is calling right now!
What? Did somebody say something?
Open your hearts! There are sisters and brothers
who need you.
Who, me? But I don't have any special talent.
We are all the talented, gifted children of God.
Look; listen; love.
I lift up my eyes and see God all around.

Opening Prayer (1 Thessalonians 5, Matthew 25)

God of light and love,
    help us walk in your light
    and live in your love.
Open our eyes,
    to see your face
    in everyone we meet.
Open our ears
    to hear your call
    as you speak and call us to serve.
Open our hearts
    to love the works of your hands,
    a world in need of your love.
Open our minds
    to understand your word and your truth this day.
Amen.

PROCLAMATION AND RESPONSE

Prayer of Confession (1 Thessalonians 5, Matthew 25)

We too often complain, O God,
    about the talents we don't have,
        instead of using the talents we do.
Release us from the voices

that counsel us that we don't have enough:
    not enough time,
    not enough money,
    not enough talents,
    not enough friends,
    not enough self-confidence.
Forgive us when we don't value
    every precious gift we are given.
Reclaim us as your people,
    that we might truly live
      as children of light,
      and as servants of love.
In Christ's mercy, we pray. Amen.

Words of Assurance (1 Thessalonians 5)

Beloved, you are all children of light
    and children of the day.
We are not of the night or of darkness.
In Christ, we are clothed with mercy and grace.
In Christ, we are forgiven!
In Christ, we are robed in faith and love,
    covered with the hope of salvation.
In Christ, salvation is ours!

Prayer of Preparation or Response to the Word (1 Thessalonians 5, Matthew 25)

Mighty God,
    wake us up!
Shine upon us with your wisdom and truth,
    that we might truly see
      all that you have given to us.
Enlighten our muddled minds,
    that we might truly understand
      your call and purpose for our lives.
Wake us up,
    that we might live continually with you
      in our sleeping and in our waking.

THANKSGIVING AND COMMUNION

Invitation to the Offering (Matthew 25)

Come forward, servants of God.
Bring your talents, your gifts.
From those to whom much has been given,
  much is expected.
From those to whom some has been given,
  some is expected.
From those to whom a little has been given,
  a little bit is still expected.
Christ calls to each of us:
"Come forward, servants of God."

Offering Prayer (Matthew 25)

God of light and love,
  receive these gifts,
  meager though they may be.
Enrich our lives with your love,
  that we may enrich your world
    with love constantly shared.
Bless and guide our paths,
  that we may hear those words:
    "Well done, good and trustworthy servant;
    enter into the joy of your master!" Amen.

SENDING FORTH

Benediction (1 Thessalonians 5)

Beloved, you are children of light!
Walk in the light of God's love!
Beloved, we are children of faith!
We go in the spirit of hope!
My friends, you are beloved of God.
Go forth with love for all!

CONTEMPORARY OPTIONS

Contemporary Gathering Words (1 Thessalonians 5, Matthew 25)

Thieves, labor pains, hidden talents, frightening bosses.
These are the dark realities of life.
But Christ's light breaks into these shadowy corners.
Let the light shine.
Let the light shine.
Let the light shine.
Precious, loved children of God,
come into the light of Christ's grace!

Praise Sentences (Psalm 123, 1 Thessalonians 5)

Lift up your eyes!
Christ's light shines forth!
The light of God shines all around!
The light of God shines all around!

NOVEMBER 23, 2008

Reign of Christ
Christ the King

Mary J. Scifres

COLOR
White or Gold

SCRIPTURE READINGS
Ezekiel 34:11-16, 20-24; Psalm 100; Ephesians 1:15-23; Matthew 25:31-46

THEME IDEAS
Being a ruler of sheep is probably not all that kingly a duty and yet it is the servant call that Christ has accepted in our lives and in our world. Today's scriptures remind us that caring selflessly is the work of Christ our King, and also the work to which we are called. Power and dominion are not gilded with jewels and palaces. Rather, power and dominion carry great responsibility. To be the name above all names is to be the servant of all humanity. To be those who claim the name "Christian" is to follow our servant-master and become servants to all in need. To see and respond to those needs are the marks of a Christian follower. To care for others, we must open our eyes and see the needs that surround us each and every day.

INVITATION AND GATHERING

Call to Worship (Psalm 100, Matthew 25)

Make a joyful noise, a noise of love and care!
Praise God with generosity and compassion!
Sing to the Lord with acts of kindness!
Give God glory with missions of mercy!
Make a joyful noise, a noise of love and care!
Praise God with justice and righteousness!

Opening Prayer (Ephesians 1, Matthew 25)

Glorious God,
    shine upon us
        with your spirit of wisdom and truth.
Enlighten our hearts.
Help us know the hope
    to which we are called.
Reveal your ways,
    that we might share hope and joy
        in all that we do and all that we say.
In the light of Christ's love, we pray. Amen.

PROCLAMATION AND RESPONSE

Prayer of Confession (Matthew 25)

God of glory,
    we do not always see your glory
        in the world around us.
When we see a person in need,
    it is not easy to look him in the eye.
When we hear a cry for help,
    it is not easy to offer her quick assurance.
When we know of a lonely prisoner,
    it is not easy to make that unannounced visit.
Forgive us when we fail to see you
    in our everyday lives.
Forgive us when we are afraid to act,
    afraid to care.

Encourage us, God of glory.
Help us see others with the eyes of compassion,
that we might be your loving presence
in the world. Amen.

Words of Assurance (Ephesians 1)
There is immeasurable greatness
in the power of God
for those who believe.
Trust in the Lord,
for God's grace is real.
In the name of Jesus Christ,
who is above all and in all,
you are forgiven!

Response to the Word/Sermon (Matthew 25)
Compassionate God,
help us show compassion
to all whom we meet.
Help us see your face:
in every hungry child,
in every tired woman,
in every disappointed man.
Help us hear your cry:
in every person who mourns,
every person who is lonely,
every person who is in agony.
Help us feel your presence,
that we might have the courage and the confidence
to act with compassion and love
everywhere we go,
and with everyone we meet. Amen.

THANKSGIVING AND COMMUNION

Invitation to the Offering (Psalm 100, Matthew 25)
Enter God's gates with thanksgiving and praise.
Come to the Lord, who is good.

Let us continue God's faithfulness
in our acts of giving and works of charity.

Offering Prayer (Matthew 25)
We offer these gifts to you:
as food and drink for a hungry world,
as clothing and shelter
for those who are naked and homeless,
as kindness and compassion
for those who are most in need of mercy.
Transform these gifts,
that they might be your hands and feet in the world.
Send us forth as your people,
that all that we do and all that we say
may be a glorious representation
of your presence in the world.
With gratitude, we pray. Amen.

SENDING FORTH

Benediction (Ezekiel 34, Matthew 25)
Seek the lost; bind up the injured.
Strengthen the weak; encourage the fainthearted.
Seek justice, but love mercy.
**And the world will know the feast of God's justice
and the grace of God's mercy.**
Amen.
Amen.

CONTEMPORARY OPTIONS

Contemporary Gathering Words (Matthew 25)
Sheep and goats are welcome here.
Saints and sinners are part of God's world.
Come; rejoice in Christ Jesus, who welcomes us all!
Come; share in his grace,
that we all might become sheep—
who feed one another,

who show compassion and love,
who offer comfort and mercy,
who give as we have received.
Come; rejoice in Christ Jesus,
who welcomes us all!

Praise Sentences (Psalm 100)
Enter this place with thankful hearts!
Make a joyful noise!
Bring shouts and songs, laughter and roars!
Make a joyful noise!
Worship our loving God!

NOVEMBER 27, 2008

Thanksgiving Day
Beverly Morrison Boke

COLOR
White

SCRIPTURE READINGS
Deuteronomy 8:7-18; Psalm 65; 2 Corinthians 9:6-15; Luke 17:11-19

THEME IDEAS
The Earth is a gift, an unearned treasure. Our task is to find harmony in our relationship to this good gift. Our actions as individuals and as communities can honor or desecrate the gift. When we forget the blessedness of this creation, we stray from what is good.

INVITATION AND GATHERING

Call to Worship: "For the Beauty of the Earth" by Barbara J. Pescan
For the beauty of the earth,
    this spinning blue green ball, yes!
Gaia, mother of everything,
    we walk gently across your back
        to come together again
            in this place,
        to remember how we can live,

to remember who we are,
to create how we will be.
Gaia, our home,
the lap in which we live—
welcome us.

Lighting the Candles
We bid welcome to all who come to give thanks this day;
who join with neighbors in glad thanksgiving,
acknowledging together the bounty of our lives.
Let this flame rise, signifying our impulse
toward the Divine.
Let us rejoice together on this day of giving thanks!

Opening Prayer
God of earth and sky,
we welcome you and thank you
for the gift of this good earth
and its many bounties.
Flow through our lives
and through this time of worship.
Blessed be!
(*Alternate ending*)
Blessed be the Lord of Creation!
(Mary J. Scifres)

PROCLAMATION AND RESPONSE

Meditation/Words of Preparation
Let us always be mindful
that the place where we stand is holy.
This planet is our home, our life, our hope.
Every breath we take receives the whole world.
Every step we take moves us through generations of life.
Matter is neither created nor destroyed;
it is changed endlessly,
and we who effect changes
are bound by our faith to consider

the potential for good and for harm in all we do.
Let us be mindful, then, of this great gift—
    which we neither made nor earned,
    conceived nor understand—
        and walk in gentleness upon the great Mother Earth.

THANKSGIVING AND COMMUNION

Congregational Liturgy: "A Harvest of Gratitude" by Percival Chubb

Once more the fields have ripened to harvest, and the fruit-ful earth has fulfilled the promise of spring.

The work of those who labor has been rewarded: They have sown and reaped, planted and gathered.

How rich and beautiful is the bounty gathered: The golden grain and clustered corn, the grapes of purple and green,

The crimson apples and yellow pears, and all the colors of orchard and garden, vineyard and field.

Season follows after season, after winter the spring, after the summer the harvest-laden autumn.

From bud to blossom, from flower to fruit, from seed to bud again, the beauty of earth unfolds.

From the harvest of the soil we are given occasion to garner a harvest of the heart and mind:

A harvest of resolve to be careful stewards of all life's gifts and opportunities.

A harvest of reverence for the wondrous power and life at work in things that grow, and in the soul.

A harvest of gratitude for every good that we enjoy, and of fellowship for all who are sustained by earth's bounty.

(© American Ethical Union, Inc., www.aeu.org)

Invitation to the Offering
From the bounty of our lives,
let us bring forth our gifts for the work of this church,
giving generously,
as we have been given to generously,
all equal children of the earth.

Offering Dedication
Let this offering support and strengthen this house.
Let these gifts be put to work in service.
Let our hearts bend toward wholeness.

SENDING FORTH

Benediction (Isaiah 55:12)
"You shall go out in joy, and be led back in peace;
the mountains and the hills before you
shall burst into song,
and all the trees of the field shall clap their hands."

CONTEMPORARY OPTIONS

Contemporary Gathering Words
From mother earth, we were formed.
From mother earth, we are fed.
From lives of bounty, we are blessed.
From homes and work, we have gathered here.
Come, eat your fill and bless our God.
The earth's bounties are given for our nourishment!
Share these gifts and bless our world.
The earth's bounties are given for all.
(Mary Scifres)

<u>Praise Sentences</u>
Thanks be for the gifts of this earth!
Thanks be for the gift of life!
Thanks be for the gifts of this earth!
Thanks be for the gift of life!
(Mary Scifres)

NOVEMBER 30, 2008

First Sunday of Advent
B. J. Beu

COLOR
Purple

SCRIPTURE READINGS
Isaiah 64:1-9; Psalm 80:1-7, 17-19; 1 Corinthians 1:3-9;
Mark 13:24-37

THEME IDEAS
God is not the kindly old man who dotes on his children
that many of us studied in Sunday school. God is the
fearsome creator who Isaiah invokes to tear open
the heavens and come down to redeem Israel. God hid
from us, we transgressed, leaving us with one angry
deity. The psalmist calls on this angry God to restore us
and save us. God has fed us with the bread of tears, but
there is hope because God is faithful. Mark's Gospel
warns us to be awake, because we know not when the
master will return. Time is short—be ready, keep awake.
The epistle reading does not readily fit this theme, but
does emphasize that the hope looked for in the Hebrew
Scriptures has been found in Christ, who strengthens us
and bestows upon us spiritual gifts.

INVITATION AND GATHERING

Call to Worship (Psalm 80)

O Lord of hosts, you have been our Shepherd.
You redeem us when we stray from your ways.
Stir up your might and come and save us.
How long will you be angry with your people?
How long will you hold our iniquities against us?
You have fed us with the bread of tears,
and given us tears to drink in full measure.
Let your hand be upon your Son,
the one you made strong to accomplish your purposes.
Restore us, O Lord God of hosts.
Let your face shine upon us, that we might be saved.

Opening Prayer (Mark 13)

God of glory,
your power darkens the skies,
your might causes the moon to grow dark.
Gather us from the four winds.
Gather us from the ends of the earth
and the ends of heaven.
Help us awaken from our slumber,
and be ready for your arrival.
Like the doorkeeper on watch,
may we be found ready
when the master of the house returns.

PROCLAMATION AND RESPONSE

Prayer of Confession (Isaiah 64)

Eternal God,
O that you would tear open the heavens
and come down.
In ages past,
you did awesome deeds
that no one expected.
You came down,

and the mountains quaked at your presence,
the nations trembled at your feet.
Rather than rejoice in our salvation,
we fell into sin.
Rather than exult in your glory,
we gave ourselves over to iniquity.
O how your anger burned against us
for our transgressions.
Let the fire of your fury
purify us of all wrong,
that we might be reshaped by your hands
into something wonderful and new. Amen.

Words of Assurance (1 Corinthians 1)
Through the grace of God, granted us in Jesus Christ,
we have been enriched in every way:
in speech and knowledge of every kind.
Through the grace of God in Christ,
we find grace and peace.

Response to the Word/Sermon (1 Corinthians 1)
The testimony of Christ
has been strengthened among us,
so that we are not lacking in any spiritual gift
as we wait for the revealing
of our Lord, Jesus Christ.
God will strengthen us to the end,
so that we may be blameless on that day.
The One who is faithful
calls us into fellowship
with Christ and with each other.

Call to Prayer (Isaiah 64)
O God, you are the potter,
we are the clay.
Mold us into new and glorious vessels,
that we may be fit for your purposes
and exhibit your glory.

You are our God;
>we are your people.
Hear our prayers of petition and thanksgiving
>as we worship you this morning.

Thanksgiving and Communion

Call to the Offering (1 Corinthians 1)
In every way,
>we have been enriched
>>through our faith in Christ Jesus.
God has granted us grace.
God has blessed us with every spiritual gift
>needed to be the body of Christ.
God has strengthened us for the journey.
Enriched by so many blessings,
>let us demonstrate our faith anew
>>as we present our gifts and offerings
>>>to the One who has so richly blessed us.

Sending Forth

Benediction (Mark 13)
Keep alert; Christ is coming soon.
>**We await God's Son.**
Keep awake; Christ is coming to us.
>**We await God's salvation.**
Be ready; Christ is among us now.
>**We go with God's blessing.**

Contemporary Options

Contemporary Gathering Words (Mark 13)
When is the Master coming?
>**No one knows the day or the hour.**
When must we be ready to receive the Lord of hosts?
>**Even now, listen for the knock on the door.**
Keep alert and be ready.
>**We await the one who brings us life.**

Praise Sentences (Psalm 80)

God restores our life.
God hears our prayers.
God saves us from our sins.
God's face shines upon us.
God restores our life.

DECEMBER 7, 2008

Second Sunday of Advent
Mary J. Scifres

COLOR
Purple

SCRIPTURE READINGS
Isaiah 40:1-11; Psalm 85:1-2, 8-13; 2 Peter 3:8-15a; Mark 1:1-8

THEME IDEAS
Advent is a time of waiting. Today, we focus on the day of righteousness that God promises. We wait with patience and perseverance to live in that time when love and faithfulness come together, when righteousness and peace dwell in harmony. Even as we wait, we prepare by being at peace in our own lives and with one another; we prepare by living in righteousness and faithfulness, as if the new heaven were already here. As December hurries along, these scriptures invite us to slow down, to reflect on peace, to listen for words of comfort, and to offer patience in a harried world.

INVITATION AND GATHERING

Call to Worship (Isaiah 40)
Tenderly calling, God speaks:
"Comfort, O comfort my people."

We wander, confused in this busy season,
lost in the mall, stuck in traffic.
Crying with love, God speaks:
"Get up to a high mountain and shout the good news!"
We climb endless hills, facing the piles of cards
unanswered, the gifts yet unwrapped.
Promising hope, God speaks:
"Every mountain shall be made low.
The uneven ground shall be leveled."
We trudge along, looking for joy
in scheduled activities, and long-held traditions.
Proclaiming love, God speaks:
"Do not fear! Here is your God!"
We walk this journey,
led by the shepherd of love.
And when we tire, we are carried in the bosom of God.
We wait with patience and anticipation,
for God is with us even now!

Opening Prayer (Isaiah 40)
Shepherding God,
guide us through this season
of anticipation and hope.
Comfort our troubled minds,
and strengthen our tired bodies.
Restore the hope this season offers,
that we might lift our voices
with strength and joy!
Straighten the crooked paths,
that we might walk in your ways.
Level the rocky ground,
that we might prepare for your arrival
in our world.
In Christ's name, we pray. Amen.

PROCLAMATION AND RESPONSE

Prayer of Confession (Isaiah 40)

God of tenderness and love,
> breathe your grace into our lives.

Forgive our wandering ways,
> and guide us along your paths of peace.

When we lose our way,
> and forget the reason and purpose of this season,
> > carry us back to you.

Lead us up to that high mountain of faith and hope,
> that we might truly proclaim:
> > "Here is our God!"

In your holy name, we pray. Amen.

Words of Assurance (Isaiah 40)

"Comfort, O comfort my people," says our God.
You have served your term. Your penalty is paid.
In the name of Jesus Christ, you are forgiven.
In the name of Jesus Christ, you are forgiven!

Response to the Word (Psalm 85, 2 Peter 3)

O Righteous One,
> let your righteousness dwell in us,
> > and cover this earth.

Let your peace rule in our hearts,
> and dwell in these lands.

Help us be patient,
> even as we persevere in hope
> > to bring to fruition
> > > your new heaven and new earth.

In Christ's name, we pray. Amen.

THANKSGIVING AND COMMUNION

The Great Thanksgiving (An Act of Preparation for Holy Communion)

The Lord be with you.
And also with you.

Come to the mountain of the Lord.
We come with hopeful hearts.
Lift up your voice with strength!
We lift our hearts and our voices to God.
Let us give thanks to the Lord our God.
It is right to give our thanks and praise.

It is right, and a good and joyful thing,
    always and everywhere to give thanks to you,
    mighty God, Comforter and Sustainer.
You formed us in your image,
    and breathed into us the breath of life.
When our constancy was like grass,
    and we wandered away from you,
    your steadfast love endured.
You delivered us from hopelessness and fear,
    made a covenant to be with us always,
    and spoke to us through your prophets and psalmists,
    who looked for that time
    when steadfast love and faithfulness would meet,
    when righteousness and peace would kiss each other.
Knowing that salvation is at hand,
    we sing of your glory,
    and rejoice in your promised coming.
And so, with your people on earth,
    and all the company of heaven,
    we praise your name
    and join their unending hymn, saying:
    Holy, holy, holy Lord, God of power and might,
    heaven and earth are full of your glory.
Hosanna in the highest.
Blessed is the one
    who comes in the name of the Lord.
Hosanna in the highest.

Holy are you, and blessed is your Promised One,
    our Lord Jesus Christ,

whom you sent in the fullness of time
to baptize us with the Holy Spirit.
You offer comfort where there is sorrow.
You speak words of tenderness where there is pain.
You make straight the crooked roads of life,
that we may walk in pathways of peace.
You level the mountains that block our way,
and you lift up the valleys that leave us in darkness.
You show us your glory,
that we may lift up our voices with strength and joy.
You come with might and with compassion.
You gather us together as your flock,
leading us, carrying us, living among us.
You came even as a servant among us,
Emmanuel, God with us,
with power and strength beyond measure.
You gave even your own life,
that we might know of your great and powerful love.

On the night in which Christ gave to us most fully,
Jesus took the bread, broke it,
and gave it to the disciples, saying:
"Take, eat, this is the bread of life, given for you.
Do this in remembrance of me."
After supper, Jesus took the cup, blessed it
and gave it to his disciples, saying:
"Drink from this, all of you."
With this living water,
Jesus proclaimed God's new covenant
of grace and mercy, steadfast love and faithfulness,
and taught us all to remember, saying:
"Do this, as often as you drink it,
in remembrance of me."
And so, in remembrance of these,
your mighty acts of love and grace,
we offer ourselves in praise and thanksgiving
as a holy and living gift.
In union with Christ's love for us,

we proclaim the mystery of faith.
Christ has died. Christ is risen.
Christ will come again.

Communion Prayer
　Pour out your Holy Spirit
　　on your servants gathered here.
　Pour out your Holy Spirit
　　on these gifts of bread and wine,
　　that we might be infused
　　　with the gift of your grace.
　Help us know you
　　and experience your nourishment,
　　even as we eat this bread
　　and drink this wine.
　Transform us to be your presence in the world,
　　even as we are redeemed and reclaimed
　　　by your great love.
　By your Spirit,
　　make us one with Christ,
　　one with each other,
　　and one in ministry to all the world,
　　until Christ comes again in final victory,
　　and we feast at the heavenly banquet.
　Through Jesus Christ and the Holy Spirit,
　　all honor and glory is yours, almighty God,
　　now and forevermore. Amen.

Giving the Bread and Cup
　(The bread and wine are given to the people, with these or other
　words of blessing.)
　The promise of Christ, living in you.
　The love of Christ, flowing through you.

SENDING FORTH

Benediction (2 Peter 3, Mark 1)
　Wait for the Lord.
　God's righteousness will appear.

In hope, we move forward with faith.
Be patient in waiting.
God is not slow, but gracious.
In gratitude, we move forward with joy.
Make a straight path.
Prepare for God.
With advent anticipation,
we journey toward Christmas!

CONTEMPORARY OPTIONS

Contemporary Gathering Words (2 Peter 3, Mark 1)
Christ is coming soon.
Prepare the way of the Lord!
Christmas is almost here.
Prepare the way of the Lord!
A new heaven and earth will appear.
Prepare the way of the Lord!

Praise Sentences (Isaiah 40, Psalm 85)
Lift up your voice with strength.
Sing of God's glory and grace!
Lift up your voice with strength.
Sing of God's glory and grace!

DECEMBER 14, 2008

Third Sunday of Advent

B. J. Beu

COLOR
Purple

SCRIPTURE READINGS
Isaiah 61:1-4, 8-11; Psalm 126; 1 Thessalonians 5:16-24;
John 1:6-8, 19-28

THEME IDEAS
The One who restores Israel brings good news: release to
the captives, help to the oppressed, and joy to the brokenhearted. The One who restored Israel's fortunes in
the time of Isaiah sent John to make straight the way of
the Messiah. Now is the time to rejoice, to pray without
ceasing, and to prepare for our salvation.

INVITATION AND GATHERING
Call to Worship (Isaiah 61)
The spirit of the Lord God is upon us:
to bring good news to the oppressed;
to bind up the brokenhearted;
to proclaim liberty to the captives;
and release to the prisoners.
The spirit of the Lord God has anointed us:
to proclaim the year of the Lord's favor;

to announce the day of vengeance of our God;
to comfort those who mourn;
and give them a garland instead of ashes,
a mantle of praise instead of a faint spirit.
Come worship the Lord who clothes us
with the garments of salvation.
Worship the Lord!

Opening Prayer (Psalm 126, Isaiah 61)
God of power and might,
	restore your people,
		that we might be like those who dream.
Fill our mouths with laughter,
	our tongues with shouts of joy.
From times of old,
	you have done great things for your people.
May we be known to the nations
	as oaks of righteousness,
	the plantings of the Lord.
We rejoice in your salvation, O God,
	and exult in your glory. Amen.

PROCLAMATION AND RESPONSE

Prayer of Confession (John 1, Isaiah 64)
Merciful God,
	how many John the Baptists,
	how many prophets of your light,
		have we ignored
			because they were not what we were looking for?
How many times have we ignored voices
	crying in the wilderness,
		"Make straight the way of the Lord."
How many times have we breathed a sigh of relief,
	and turned our backs on your messengers,
	because they did not speak the message
		we expected to hear?
Help us hear anew,

the cry of those who would lead us to Christ.
Tune our ears to your heralds,
    that we might also testify to your light. Amen.

Words of Assurance (1 Thessalonians 5:23-24)
May the God of peace sanctify you completely.
And may your whole spirit, soul, and body be kept
    blameless
    at the coming of our Lord Jesus Christ.
The one who calls you is faithful.
It is the Lord who will do this.

Response to the Word/Sermon (1 Thessalonians 5:20-22, John 1)
"Do not despise the words of prophets,
    but test everything;
hold fast to what is good;
    abstain from every form of evil."
As children of the light,
    in all things bear testimony to the light,
    that others may believe through you.

Call to Prayer (1 Thessalonians 5:16-19)
"Rejoice always, pray without ceasing,
    give thanks in all circumstances;
    for this is the will of God in Christ Jesus for you.
Do not quench the Spirit,"
    but in all things
        let your prayers be made known to God.
Let us pray.

THANKSGIVING AND COMMUNION

Call to the Offering (1 Corinthians 1)
As those whom Christ has sanctified to his purposes,
    those whose hopes and dreams have been restored,
        let our deeds reflect the light we have been given.
May our offerings express the joy and exultation
    we feel for the gift of our salvation
        through Christ Jesus, our Lord.

SENDING FORTH

Benediction (Mark 13)

Be free from the bondage
that has imprisoned our spirits.
Christ is our light and our salvation.
Be free of the futility and despair
that has driven out our hope.
Christ is our light and our salvation.
Be free of the darkness
that has shrouded us from God.
Christ is our light and our salvation.

CONTEMPORARY OPTIONS

Contemporary Gathering Words (Psalm 126)

What are your dreams, people of God?
To be filled with laughter;
to cry with joy, not with sorrow.
What are your hopes, people of God?
To be free of the chains that bind us;
to shout with thanksgiving, not with anguish.
Rejoice, people of God; here and now,
God makes our hopes and dreams come true.

Praise Sentences (John 1)

Christ is our light.
Rejoice in God's love.
Christ is our light.
Rejoice in God's salvation.
Christ is our light.
Christ is our light.
Christ is our light.

DECEMBER 21, 2008

Fourth Sunday of Advent
Mary J. Scifres

COLOR
Purple

SCRIPTURE READINGS
2 Samuel 7:1-11, 16; Luke 1:47-55; Romans 16:25-27;
Luke 1:26-38

THEME IDEAS
Glorifying God begins with humility on our part. For
Mary to receive the gift and challenge of bearing the Christ
child, she first listened to God's message with confusion
and doubt. With humility, she asked, "How can this be?"
With faith, she accepted the prophetic promise and
answered God's call, saying, "Here am I ... let it be." As
Christmas nears, we are challenged to receive God's gifts
with careful thought, with humility, and with faith. We are
given a great opportunity as the body of Christ to continue
bearing Christ for the world. In doing so, we assist the in-
breaking of God's realm and glorify God with our love.

INVITATION AND GATHERING
Greeting (Luke 1)
Greetings, favored ones!
The Lord is with you!

Greetings, in the name of Christ.
God is with us now!

Psalm of Praise (Luke 1)
Our souls magnify the Lord!
Our spirits rejoice in God our Savior!
The Mighty One has done great things for us.
Holy is God's name!
God's mercy is ever near, from generation to generation.
God's strength scatters the proud,
but lifts the humble of heart.
God's love fills us up, nourishing our hungry souls.
God's grace has called us here,
strengthening our lives of faith.

Opening Prayer (Luke 1)
Mighty God,
pour out your Holy Spirit
on all of us gathered here.
As we follow in Mary's footsteps,
open our hearts,
that we might be filled with your goodness
and your love;
live in us,
that we might bear the Christ light
for all to see;
overshadow us with your presence,
that we might truly be blessed
and offer your blessing of love to the world.

PROCLAMATION AND RESPONSE

Prayer of Confession (Luke 1)
Savior God,
shine upon us with your grace.
Forgive us when we align ourselves
with the proud and the mighty.
Guide us to walk with those

who are poor and weak.
Forgive us when we yearn for riches and glory.
Guide us to yearn for justice and righteousness.
Remember us with mercy.
Help us live as the household of faith
    you would have us be.
Help us live according to your gospel
    and trust that all things are possible
        in your love.
In Christ's saving grace, we pray. Amen.

Words of Assurance (Luke 1)

Rejoice! God has looked with favor
    upon the powerless and the lowly.
Christ has come to redeem us from our sin.
The Spirit has strengthened us
    with the power of grace and love.
In the mercy of the Triune God, we are forgiven!

THANKSGIVING AND COMMUNION

Invitation to the Offering (Luke 1)

Remembering the great things God has done for us,
    we are now invited to return these symbols
        of our gratitude to God.
Even as we offer small things,
    when done with the love of Christ in our hearts,
    our offerings are transformed into mighty miracles.
Let us fill the hungry with our gifts.
Let us lift up the lowly with our compassion.
Let us remember a world in need.
With mercy and love,
    let us offer ourselves and our gifts.

Prayer of Thanksgiving (Luke 1)

Just as our souls magnify the Lord,
    may our offerings glorify God.
Surely, we are blessed.

We rejoice in the mercy that you have shown
from generation to generation.
We remember the powerful promise you bring:
hope to the hopeless and strength to the weak.
With joy, we pray in gratitude and praise. Amen.

SENDING FORTH

Benediction (Romans 16, Luke 1)
May God strengthen you according to the gospel.
May the proclamation of Jesus Christ
dwell in your hearts and in your lives.
And may the power of the Holy Spirit
be with you now and forevermore. Amen.

CONTEMPORARY OPTIONS

Contemporary Gathering Words (Luke 1)
God looks kindly on us when we are at our lowest.
Rejoice in God our Savior!
God has done great things for us in times past.
God will do great things for us in days to come.
Rejoice in God our Savior!
Christ's mercy is upon us,
offering hope in times of despair.
Rejoice in God our Savior!
Christ's love has made us whole.
Rejoice in God our Savior!
The Spirit's power disarms our pride
and prejudice.
Rejoice in God our Savior!
The Spirit's power strengthens our mercy
and compassion.
Rejoice in God our Savior!
Even as we are filled this day,
may we go forth to nourish a world in need.
Rejoice in God our Savior!

Praise Sentences

O magnify the Lord!
God is worthy to be praised!
O magnify the Lord!
God is worthy to be praised!

DECEMBER 24, 2008

Christmas Eve
B. J. Beu

COLOR
White

SCRIPTURE READINGS
Isaiah 9:2-7; Psalm 96; Titus 2:11-14; Luke 2:1-20

THEME IDEAS
This is a night for rejoicing, a night to sing a new song to God, a night to celebrate the wondrous salvation offered through the birth of Jesus. Isaiah proclaims, "The people who walked in darkness / have seen a great light" (Isaiah 9:2). This light has been brought forth through a child who will rule with justice and righteousness. Echoing this theme, the psalmist calls us to sing our praises for God's salvation. And Luke recounts the birth narrative of the Christ child, whom we worship this night with the angels and shepherds.

INVITATION AND GATHERING

Call to Worship (Isaiah 9, Psalm 96)
The people who walked in darkness have seen a great light.
Too long have we dwelt in darkness.
Too long have our eyes beheld only shadow.
Those who lived in a land of deep darkness—

on them light has shined.
Your light dazzles our vision, O God.
Who will lead us into the dawn of your saving love?
A child has been born for us.
God's own Son has been given to us.
We will call him Wonderful Counselor, Mighty God,
Everlasting Father, Prince of Peace.
His authority shall grow continually, and there shall be
endless peace for the throne of David.
Let the trees of the forest sing for joy!
Let heaven and nature sing.
The zeal of the Lord of hosts will do this.

Opening Prayer (Isaiah 9, Luke 2)
Prepare our hearts, O God,
to receive the Christ child once more.
Shine your light
into the darkness of our world.
Shine your glory
into the shadows of our lives.
Like the shepherds in the fields,
who watched over their flocks by night,
may we be stirred into action
by the singing of the angelic chorus.
Overcome our fear, Holy One,
and inspire us to leave our flocks,
and seek the Christ child this night.
Prepare our hearts, O God,
to behold your precious gift
in awe and wonder.

PROCLAMATION AND RESPONSE

Christmas Eve Litany (Luke 2)
In the midst of a dark, night sky, a star beckons:
Rise up, shepherd, and follow.
In the quiet of evening rest, an angel proclaims:
Rise up, shepherd, and follow.

In the midst of our loneliness and pain, God calls:
Rise up, children, and follow.
With the promise of new life, Christ is born to save us:
Rise up, children, and follow.

Response to the Word/Sermon (Luke 2)
There was no room at the inn for God's servants.
But there is room in our hearts for God's word.
There was amazement in the fields
when the angels proclaimed the Messiah's birth.
**And there is wonder in our hearts
as we receive this news once again.**
In her heart, Mary treasured the words of the shepherds.
**In our hearts, we treasure Mary's love
and the story of our savior's birth.**

Call to Prayer (Psalm 96, Isaiah 9)
Christ judges the people with equity.
Let the heavens be glad, and let the Earth rejoice.
Christ judges the world with righteousness
and the peoples with truth.
**Let us offer our prayers of thanksgiving to the child
who is our Wonderful Counselor and Prince of Peace.**
Let us pray.

THANKSGIVING AND COMMUNION

Call to the Offering (1 Corinthians 1)
What greater gift could we receive
than the gift of God's own child—
a child who is our light and our salvation?
We, who have received so much,
are called to join the shepherds
in sharing our joy;
we are challenged to join the Magi
in offering our gifts to the Christ child.
Come; let us give out of our abundance.

SENDING FORTH

Benediction (Isaiah 9)
Walk in darkness no longer.
Christ is our light and our salvation.
Treasure the gift of Jesus' birth.
Christ is our light and our salvation.
Linger in the echo of the angelic chorus.
Christ is our light and our salvation.

CONTEMPORARY OPTIONS

Contemporary Gathering Words (Isaiah 9)
Jesus is born this very night.
Love is born this very hour.
Hope is born from the depth of despair.
Let us sing with the angels
and dance with the shepherds.
Jesus is born this very night.
Love is born this very hour.

Praise Sentences
Jesus is born.
God's light has come!
Jesus is born.
God's light is here!
Jesus is born.
God's light is all around us.
Jesus is born. Alleluia!

DECEMBER 28, 2008

First Sunday after Christmas
Mary J. Scifres

COLOR
White

SCRIPTURE READINGS
Isaiah 61:10–62:3; Psalm 148; Galatians 4:4-7; Luke 2:22-40

THEME IDEAS
The glory of God's extraordinary salvation through Christ Jesus is juxtaposed with the presentation at temple of a young Jewish boy in an ordinary Jewish ritual. Even as his family participates in this common custom, the uncommon breaks in. Simeon proclaims Jesus to be the long-awaited Messiah, the salvation for which Simeon waited. Anna praises God for this young child in whom she sees "the redemption of Jerusalem" (Luke 2:38). Christmas is a reminder that our extraordinary God breaks into our ordinary world, our ordinary lives, and our ordinary traditions.

INVITATION AND GATHERING

Call to Worship (Psalm 148, Luke 2)
Men and women, gather together
and praise the Lord above!
Praise we bring to the light of God,
shining upon our lives!

Young and old, gather together
and praise the One in our midst!
Praise we bring to the light of the world,
Christ Jesus come to earth!

Opening Prayer (Luke 2, Galatians 4)
Light of the world,
shine in our lives this day.
As we hear your word and worship,
help us grow in the strength and wisdom
of your love.
Send the Spirit of Christ into our hearts,
that we might truly know
that we are your children,
and that you are our God.
In Christ's name, we pray. Amen.

PROCLAMATION AND RESPONSE

Litany of Joy (Isaiah 61, Galatians 4, Luke 2)
Do not keep silent. Shout aloud, for Christ is born.
Rejoice in the Lord, for Christ has come among us!
Christ has clothed us with the garment of salvation.
We are covered with robes of righteousness.
We are adopted as children and heirs of God,
shining with love for the world.
Let your light shine, that all may know:
Christ is born; God is here; love is with us now!

Prayer of Preparation (Galatians 4, Luke 2)
Shine on us with your wisdom
as we listen and receive your word.
Let your word take root and grow in our lives,
that we may be filled
with your wisdom and righteousness.
Let your Spirit rule in our hearts,
that we may live as children
who shine with the light and love of God.

Response to the Word (Luke 2)

Miraculous God,
thank you for the extraordinary gift of Christmas.
Help us live with Christmas joy and Christlike wisdom
throughout the year ahead.
Work in our ordinary lives
with your extraordinary power,
that we might be children who truly glorify you.
With Christmas joy and New Year hope, we pray. Amen.

THANKSGIVING AND COMMUNION

Invitation to the Offering (Luke 2)

When the time had come,
Mary and Joseph brought Jesus to the temple,
dedicated him to God,
and offered gifts of sacrifice to God
in thanksgiving and praise.
In honor and memory of that ancient tradition,
we come to this time of offering.
This is the time to dedicate ourselves to God
and to offer our gifts of thanksgiving and praise.

Offering Prayer (Luke 2)

Gracious God,
thank you for these gifts
and for the gift of your Son.
As we offer these gifts to you,
we also offer you our lives.
Bless these gifts,
that they may be signs of your redemption
and your hope to a world in need.
Bless our lives,
that we may shine with your glory
and light up the world with your love.
In Christ's name, we pray. Amen.

SENDING FORTH

Benediction (Isaiah 61, Luke 2)

Go in peace, for we have seen the salvation of God.
We go with joy, for Christ has clothed us with love.

CONTEMPORARY OPTIONS

Contemporary Gathering Words (Luke 2)

Christmas has come.
The New Year awaits.
Let us gather, remembering the gift of Christ,
    even as we look with hope
        toward a year of new beginnings.
Let us worship, rejoicing in the gift of Christmas,
    even as we pray for Spirit-filled wisdom
        to guide our new year.

(Or)

Contemporary Gathering Words (Luke 2)

Even in an ordinary birth, in a humble stable,
an extraordinary miracle occurred.
    We yearn for God's miracles today.
Even in an ordinary religious tradition,
extraordinary prophets proclaimed Christ's purpose
in our world.
    We yearn for God's miracles today.
There is nothing ordinary about our extraordinary God.
    We yearn for God's miracles today.
There is nothing ordinary about our lives
when we are guided by God's extraordinary Spirit.
    We yearn for God's miracles today.
Ordinary miracles and extraordinary gifts
are all around us.
    We yearn for God's miracles today.
Look and rejoice! God's miracles are all around.

Praise Sentences

Praise the Lord of heaven and earth!
    Praise the Lord of heaven and earth!

CONTRIBUTORS

Erik J. Alsgaard, a clergy member of the Detroit Annual Conference, serves as the Director of Communications for the Baltimore-Washington Conference (as of 2006).

Laura Jaquith Bartlett is a United Methodist music minister in Oregon, where she lives with her husband and two daughters, all of whom enjoy Scandinavian folk dancing.

B. J. Beu is pastor of Fox Island United Church of Christ, near Gig Harbor, Washington. A graduate of Boston University and Pacific Lutheran University, Beu has chaired the worship committee for the Pacific Northwest Annual Conference of the United Church of Christ, and was a member of the worship planning team for the Fellowship of Methodists in Music and Worship Arts National Convocation in Dearborn, Michigan.

Robert Blezard left twenty-five years of writing and editing to be a minister of Word and Sacrament in the Evangelical Lutheran Church in America. His congregation now has a really good monthly newsletter. He serves Trinity Lutheran Church, Arendtsville, Pennsylvania.

Beverly Morrison Boke (Buffy) happily serves the Unitarian Universalist Fellowship of the Peninsula in Newport News, Virginia, where she lives with her husband, Nick.

Mary Petrina Boyd is pastor of Coupeville United Methodist Church on Whidbey Island, Washington. She spends alternate summers working as an archaeologist in Jordan.

John A. Brewer serves as pastor of Faith United Methodist Church in Issaquah, Washington. Now in his thirty-fifth year of ministry, John is chair of the Conference Board of Discipleship.

Joanne Carlson Brown has the joy of being both a local church pastor at United Church in University Place, Washington (a joint United Methodist–United Church of Christ Congregation) and an adjunct professor in the School of Theology and Ministry at Seattle University. She journeys through life with her wee Westie, Thistle.

S. Kasey Crosby has served as local pastor for ten years in the Kansas West Conference of The United Methodist Church.

Shelley Cunningham is a pastor at Transfiguration Lutheran Church (Evangelical Lutheran Church of America), Bloomington, Minnesota, and a writer in the communications office at Luther Seminary, St. Paul.

Rebecca J. Kruger Gaudino is an ordained minister in the United Church of Christ who teaches part-time at the University of Portland and also writes for the church.

Jamie D. Greening pastors in Port Orchard, Washington, where he lives with his family.

Hans Holznagel, a member of Archwood United Church of Christ, Cleveland, Ohio, has served for over twenty years in the national ministries of the United Church of Christ as a journalist, mission interpretation specialist, and administrator.

M. Anne Burnette Hook is a deacon in the Memphis Annual Conference and is currently serving as Minister of Music and Worship at Christ United Methodist Church in Franklin, Tennessee.

Sara Dunning Lambert is a child of God who is privileged to be a wife, mother, and nurse. She is also the worship coordinator at Bear Creek United Methodist Church in Woodinville, Washington.

Bryan Schneider-Thomas is pastor of Amble United Methodist Church near Howard City, Michigan, and also serves churches as a consultant in art and architecture.

Mary J. Scifres serves as a consultant in leadership, worship, and evangelism from her Gig Harbor home near Seattle, where she and her husband, B. J., reside with their young son, Michael. Her books include *The United Methodist Music and Worship Planner* and its ecumenical counterpart *Prepare!,* and the worship evangelism book *Searching for Seekers.*

SCRIPTURE INDEX

Genesis
1:1–2:4a 110, 111–12
2:15-17 30–34
6:11-22 119
7:24 119
8:14-19 119
12:1-4a 36–39
12:1-9 124–29
18:1-15 130
21:8-21 135–38
22:1-14 140
24:34-38, 42-49, 58-67 144–46
25:19-34 148
28:10-19a 152–55
29:15-28 156–57
32:22-31 161–64
37:1-4, 12-28 . . . . 165, 167
45:1-15 169–72

Exodus
1:8–2:10 174–77
3:1-15 178–81
12:1-4, 5-10, 11-14 60
12:1-14 183–84
14:19-31 187–90
15:1b-11, 20-21 . . . . . 187–88, 190
16:2-15 191–93
17:1-7 . . . . 41–42, 44, 195–97
20:1-4, 7-9, 12-20 . . . . 199, 201
24:12-18 19
32:1-14 204
33:12-23 208–10

Deuteronomy
8:7-18 236
34:1-12 213

Joshua
3:7-17 218–19
24:1-3a, 14-25 . . . 221–22, 224–25

Judges
4:1-7 226

1 Samuel
16:1-13 . . . . 46, 48

2 Samuel
7:1-11, 16 257

Psalms
8 . . . . 110, 113
13 140
16 74–77
17:1-7, 15 161–64
19 199–203
22 65–67
23 . . . . 46–47, 85–86, 88
27:1, 4-9 15–17
29 . . . . 6, 8–9
31:1-5, 15-16 89–90
31:9-16 . . . . 55, 57
32 . . . . 30–32, 34
33:1-12 . . . . 124–25, 127–29
40:1-11 10–13
45:10-17 144–47
46 . . . . 119, 122–23

(Psalms—cont.)

47 99–103
51:1-17 .... 25–26, 28–29
65 236
66:8-20 .... 95–96, 98
72:1-7, 10-14 1
78:1-4, 12-16 .... 195, 197
78:1-7 221
80:1-7, 17-19 ...... 241–42, 245
85:1-2, 8-13 246
86:1-10, 16-17 ... 135–36, 138–39
90:1-6, 13-17 .... 213–14, 216–17
95 41
96 .... 262, 264
99 ...... 19–20, 24, 208–10, 212
100 .... 231–33, 235
104:24-34, 35b 104
105:1-6, 16-22, 45b 165
105:1-6, 23-26, 45c 178–79,
181–82
105:1-6, 37-45 191–94
105:1-11, 45b 156, 159
106:1-6, 19-23 204–7
107:1-7, 33-37 .... 218, 220
116:1-2, 12-19 .... 130, 133
116:1-4, 12-19 ... 60, 64, 78, 80, 84
118:1-2, 14-24 70–73
118:1-2, 19-29 55–58
119:105-12 148–51
121 36–39
123 .... 226–27, 130
124 .... 174–75, 177
126 .... 253–54, 256
130 .... 50, 52–53
131 .... 114–15, 118
133 169–73
139:1-12, 23-24 152–54
148 266
149 183–86

Isaiah

9:1-4 15–18
9:2-7 262–65

40:1-11 .... 246–48, 252
42:1-9 6–8
49:1-7 .... 10, 13
49:8-16a 114, 116, 118
50:4-9a 55
52:13–53:12 65–66
60:1-6 1
61:1-4, 8-11 253–54
61:10–62:3 266–68
64:1-9 241–43

Ezekiel

34:11-16, 20-24 .... 231, 234
37:1-14 .... 50–51, 53

Joel

2:1-2, 12-17 .... 25–26, 28

Matthew

2:1-12 1
3:13-17 .... 6, 9
4:1-11 .... 30–33, 35
4:12-23 15–18
6:1-6, 16-21 25
6:24-34 114–18
7:21-29 119–22
9:9-13, 18-26 124–29
9:35–10:8 (9-23) 130–32
10:24-39 135–37
10:40-42 140–43
11:16-19, 25-30 144–47
13:1-9, 18-23 148–51
13:24-30, 36-43 ..... 152, 154–55
13:31-33, 44-52 156–59
14:13-21 161–63
14:22-33 .... 165, 167–68
15:10-20, 21-28 169
16:13-20 .... 174, 176–77
16:21-28 178–82
17:1-9 .... 19–20, 24
18:15-20 183–85
18:21-35 187
20:1-16 191–94

(Matthew—cont.)

21:1-11 55–56
21:23-32 195–96
21:33-46 . . . . 199, 202–3
22:1-14 204–5
22:15-22 208–12
22:34-46 . . . . 213, 215–17
23:1-12 . . . . 218, 220
25:1-13 . . . . 221–22, 224–25
25:14-30 226–30
25:31-46 231–34
26:14–27:66 55–56
27 68
27:1-2 67
27:3-10 67
27:15-24 68
27:26-31 68
27:32-37 68
27:50-51 69
28:16-20 110–12

Mark

1:1-8 . . . . 246, 251–52
13:24-37 . . . . 241–42, 244
15:33-34 69
15:35-36 69

Luke

1:26-38 257–60
1:47-55 257–60
2:1-14, 15-20 262–64
2:22-40 266–69
17:11-19 236
22:39-53 67
22:54b-62 67
23:35, 39-43 68
24:13-35 . . . . 78–80, 83–84
24:44-53 99

John

1:6-8, 19-28 253–56
1:29-42 . . . . 10–11, 14
3:1-17 36–38

4:5-42 41–45
7:37-39 104
9:1-41 46–49
10:1-10 . . . . 85–86, 88
11:1-45 . . . . 50, 52–53
13:1-17, 31b-35 60–64
14:1-14 . . . . 89, 94
14:15-21 . . . . 95–96, 98
18:1–19:42 . . . . 65, 67–68
20:1-18 70–73
20:19-31 74–77

Acts of the Apostles

1:1-11 99
2:1-21 104
2:14a, 22-32 . . . . 74–75, 77
2:14a, 36-41 78
2:42-47 . . . . 85, 87
7:55-60 89
10:34-43 . . . . 6, 8–9, 70–73
17:22-31 . . . . 95, 98

Romans

1:16-17 119
3:22b-28, 29-31 119
4:1-5, 13-17 36
4:13-25 . . . . 124–25, 129
5:1-8 130–32
5:1-11 41
5:12-19 . . . . 30–32, 34–35
6:1b-11 . . . . 135, 137
6:12-23 . . . . 140, 142
7:15-25a 144–47
8:1-11 148–50
8:6-11 . . . . 50–51, 53–54
8:12-25 152–55
8:26-39 156–58
9:1-5 . . . . 161, 163–64
10:5-15 165–66
11:1-2a, 29-32 169–71
12:1-8 . . . . 174, 176–77
12:9-21 178–81
13:8-14 183–86

(Romans—cont.)
14:1-12 187–90
16:25-27 .... 257, 260

1 Corinthians
1:1-9 10–14
1:3-9 .... 241, 243–44
1:10-18 .... 15, 18
4:1-5 .... 114, 116–17
11:23-26 60–64
12:3b-13 104

2 Corinthians
5:20b–6:10 25–28
9:6-15 236
13:11-13 110–13

Galatians
4:4-7 266–67

Ephesians
1:15-23 .... 99–103, 231–33
3:1-12 1
5:8-14 46–49

Philippians
1:21-30 191–94
2:1-13 .... 195–96, 198
2:5-11 55–56
3:4b-14 199–202
4:1-9 204–7

Colossians
3:1-4 70–73

1 Thessalonians
1:1-10 .... 208–10, 212
2:1-8 .... 213, 215
2:9-13 218–19
4:13-18 .... 221–23, 225
5:1-11 226–30
5:16-24 .... 253, 255

Titus
2:11-14 262

Hebrews
10:16-25 65

1 Peter
1:3-9 74–77
1:17-23 .... 78–79, 84
2:2-10 .... 85, 89–90, 92–93
2:19-25 .... 85, 87
3:13-22 95

2 Peter
1:16-21 .... 19–20, 24
3:8-15a 246, 248, 251–52

Communion Liturgies
Epiphany
or Transfiguration 19
Gen 2–3, Rom 5, Matt 4 30
Holy Thursday 60
Great Thanksgiving 78, 246
Romans 5 130

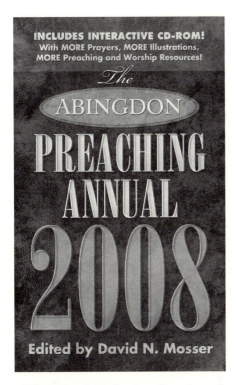

INCLUDES INTERACTIVE CD-ROM!
With MORE Prayers, MORE Illustrations,
MORE Preaching and Worship Resources!

The
ABINGDON
PREACHING
ANNUAL
2008

Edited by David N. Mosser

Preachers have long turned to *The Abingdon Preaching Annual* for help with the central task of their ministry: sermon preparation. The 2008 edition of the *Annual* continues this fine tradition with lectionary-based and topical sermons for flexibility in choice, additional lectionary commentary, and worship aids for every sermon. The CD-ROM, included with every book, provides classical and contemporary affirmations and prayers, plus hyperlinked planning aids such as bibliographical references, additional sermon illustrations, and the full lectionary texts for each Sunday. *The Abingdon Preaching Annual* is now one of the most comprehensive and useful resources for sermon preparation that you will find on the market today.

"Commendations to Abingdon Press for offering two fresh ecumenical resources for pastors."

For *The Abingdon Preaching Annual*—"Anyone who dares proclaim a holy word week in and week out soon realizes that creative inspiration for toe-shaking sermons quickly wanes. Multitasking pastors who are wise seek out resources that multiply their own inductive initiatives."

For *The Abingdon Worship Annual*—"Not only the sermon but also the whole service dares to be toe-shaking . . . and the *Worship Annual* is a reservoir of resources in that direction."

—The Reverend Willard E. Roth, Academy of Parish Clergy President, *Sharing the Practice: The Journal of the Academy of Parish Clergy*

 Abingdon Press